7

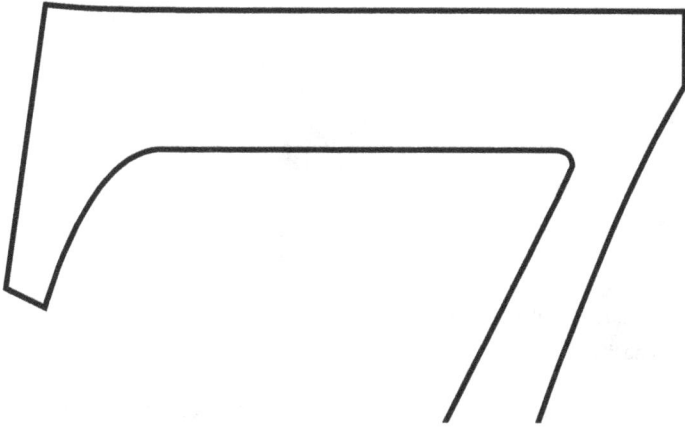

FIGURES TO SUCCESS

*Finding your Sales Excellence
in 365 days*

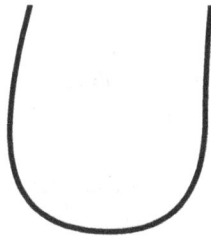

CHRIS LACHARITY

THE ULTIMATE PUBLISHING HOUSE (UPH) US HEADQUARTERS
P.O. Box 1204, Cypress, Texas, U.S.A. 77410

Canadian Office: 205 Glen Shields Avenue, Toronto, Ontario, Canada L4K 2B0
Telephone: 647-883-1758

7FigurestoSuccessbook.com

www.ultimatepublishinghouse.com
E-mail: info@ultimatepublishinghouse.com
US OFFICE: Ordering Information

Quantity Sales: COMPANIES, ORGANIZATIONS, INSTITUTIONS, AND INDUSTRY PUBLICATIONS.

Quantity discounts are available on bulk purchases of this book for reselling, subscription incentives, gifts, sponsorship, fundraising and educational purposes, including orders for college textbook or course-adoption use. Unique books or book excerpts can also be fashioned to suit special needs such as private labeling with your logo on the cover and/or with a message printed on the second page of the book. For further information, please contact our Special Sales Department at Ultimate Publishing House.

Please contact Ultimate Publishing House Tel: 647-883-1758

7 Figures to Success - By Chris Lacharity ISBN-978-1-7325389-1-7

DEDICATION

I dedicate this book to my mother. You gave me life, a sense of humor, and confidence. Without confidence, I would not be able to achieve anything I have, and for that, I owe you everything. You provided me with one of the most interesting and diverse upbringings, exposing me to powerful figures, millionaires, artists, builders, hippies etc., but most of all—you exposed me to people who were kind, caring, and exciting. No matter what life threw at me, you convinced me that I could accomplish anything. I love you for it and cherish every minute that we have together.

ACKNOWLEDGEMENTS

To Tony Greco, thanks for being an influential part of my success and fitness goals. You inspired me to write this book and shoot for the stars. You are a huge supporter and I appreciate your energy every day. You are already hugely successful but I think you're just getting started. Your enthusiasm is contagious and my life has drastically improved with you in it. Thank you for everything you have done for me, really! You're a great friend and an absolute bull in the gym. Just when I think I'm catching up, you turn it up even higher!

And to my sister, I am thankful for you always being "a sister" my entire life, and also for helping me run my business. You will be a fantastic agent and your love of people will be the secret to your success. Also, thank you for giving me two beautiful nieces and an adorable nephew.

I would like to acknowledge a few people I refer to throughout my book.

My uncle, John Lacharity, for being cool in every sense of the word. For being honest and dependable, which was so important to have growing up. You exposed me to many exciting aspects of life I may have never ended up enjoying otherwise. You have more to do with my success than you will ever give yourself credit for. I've always been extremely proud to call you my uncle.

My Aunt Pat and my Aunt Judy, both with extreme cool factor, have been a large part of my growth as a person and as a man. What I expect in a woman and how I respect them is owed to both of you. Pat, you put this goal of earning $1 Million a year in my head, so I hold you responsible for that and thank you from the bottom of my heart for all that you have done for me—which is more than you realize, I'm sure. I love you both and have always felt a deep connection to the both of you for as long as I can remember.

Donald Abraham, thank you for being the mentor that I needed for the bulk of my career. You taught me so much and you were such a reliable source of information. You are still my go-to when I'm in a pinch. Thank you for all the love and support that you and Alana have given me over the years. You are both truly like family to me.

Michael Smith, I mention what you have meant to me in the book and want to reinforce that I wouldn't be this cocky kid with huge aspirations if it weren't for you. You were truly my idol growing up and still are.

And a few more people I cherish:

My grandmother, Mary Helferty, who I barely remember, but have felt a loving presence from my whole life. I believe that we all have a path to follow which you have guided me on. I know that you're watching when nobody else is, and this has kept me humble, honest, and kind.

Jim and Brenda, you brought our massive family together throughout the years and opened your home to all of us, which has given myself and I'm sure many of my cousins – whom I adore – a sense of security when we may have needed it. You are all I know of a successful couple, which shows me it's possible.

My good friend Jules Alter, I miss you every day. I can't believe that you're gone, but I thank you for all the laughter and joy that you brought into my life during the time you were in it. You reminded me daily not to take myself so seriously. Laughter, truly is the best medicine.

Monica, you always believed in me and encouraged my dreams. You had faith that I could do all the things I spoke of and I thank you for that support. You have been a big part of my career in many ways and I want to thank you for listening to over 10 years' worth of real estate stories. You have a brilliant law career ahead of you and I know that you'll be incredible at it. You taught me so much during our time together and I can only hope that I did the same for you. I have no idea where we will be when this is published, but wherever you are, I hope most of all that you are happy. You are the most loving soul that I have encountered and you deserve nothing but the best. You're gorgeous inside and out and I'll never forget you. "A reason, a season, a lifetime."

John Huff and Donald Thom, two incredible guys to have in my life growing up. John teaching me how to throw a perfect spiral and set up fool proof football plays; Donald telling me stories that I have no idea are true or not to this day. I sure loved hearing them, though I still can't tell if you're serious that you wrestled lions at the Quebec zoo.

Marilyn Wilson, you introduced me to this crazy business and have made it possible for me to achieve my dreams. Thank you for all that you do, you are truly the best of the best and I'm flattered you saw something similar in me. You don't give yourself enough credit. I don't think anyone will achieve what you have in this city, yet you strive for more. You're my kind of people.

My uncle Greg, as I write this you are in the hospital not doing well at all and I can only hope and pray by some miracle that you get to read this and recover against all odds. I love you and you have raised two beautiful daughters who make me realize how important it is to have immediate family. They are so in love with you as their father. Its a beautiful thing to watch. I really enjoyed our chat when I stayed behind the other night by your hospital bed.

You perked right up and your eyes got bright as we spoke of boxing and fights we got into when we were younger. It's funny how we remember them with such detail. You're so proud of your dad/my grandfather being the toughest guy we knew. I tested you to see how awake you were and asked who my grandfather famously knocked out. "Archie Moore", you said right away! "He fought Mohamed Ali you know?" I said, "Yes, I know…" What a great family I come from I thought, I wouldn't have it any other way. I pray for you Greg.

Ben and Gaetano, two of my best friends who gave me the honour of being their best men in each of their weddings this summer. I know we are all busy but I so value that we take the time when we can to just hang out and laugh. You're both great friends, husbands to your wives and fathers to your children and I appreciate you daily. Thank you for sticking by my side through the good times and the bad.

My Cap Cana crew! Tony, Tony, Gino, Val, Dino, Matt and Bruce you guys are incredible!! What a life we have! I couldn't dream of a better one at times. Thank you for your support and friendship. See you on the beach. I hope all our beach houses are on the same one!

My pug Enzo, the most adorable and loyal pet anyone could ask for. I couldn't imagine the last decade without you and I hope for at least a decade more. Our morning walks are my favorite part of my day.

TABLE OF CONTENTS

NOT YOUR AVERAGE
"SALES" BOOK

The best advice I can give anyone
who desires sales excellence is to
give you the direct—no holds barred—
insights on what you need to do.

CHRIS LACHARITY

A re you ready for a life-changing year?

It's no coincidence you are reading this. Be prepared, because the information I will share with you is direct, precise, and at times a bit hardcore. If you want to experience superior sales results over the next 12 months, then you will need a process to move you from where you are right now so you can achieve the goals of your dreams.

You may be wondering, *who are you, Chris Lacharity, to tell me anything*?

I am grateful I have already achieved a large amount of success. I know I have a lot of value I can bring to the table and I want to share that with you.

I am still working on the biggest goal of my life. And that makes this the best time for me to put the strategies I use—my real-time actions, my triumphs and lessons—together, all in one place.

I am not coy. I am the first to admit I want to make money and that proclamation in itself lends some authenticity.

Money is often the yardstick by which success is measured. So, whether in sales, real estate, or in any other area, if you are doing what you love and the money doesn't matter, it is an extremely valuable thing to track.

The best business success stories come from people who know that money results from your desire to help your customers and the people you work for. I represent people who either buy or sell homes in the luxury market in the Ottawa area, in Canada.

My niche requires me to bring my A-game every single day. But that story would be the same if my niche was cookie-cutter suburban developments. It takes balance, dedication, a conquering mindset that is supported by massive action to get things done.

It's a simple concept (but not easy, and that's where I come in) and once you develop the discipline to follow my *7 Figures to Success* (where you allow no room for exceptions to your process) you will find you achieve your sales goals; whether it's $250K, $500K, or even $1M. You will be driven to succeed and what may have been a fleeting thought becomes your reality. And that my friend is very exciting.

HOW I ARRIVED AT "THIS" MOMENT

Help others achieve their dreams
and you will achieve yours.

———————————

LES BROWN

The biggest event of my childhood is when my parents divorced. I was very young and instead of being the disaster most experience, their divorce was somewhat more of a blessing. I have always felt as if I had the best of both worlds.

At the time, my mother was broke and cool; and my father was wealthy but strict and quite square. I am who I am largely because of my mother. She is a career artist with an interesting group of friends. My experiences have been very rich and I have learned many of life's lessons in their company. I would not trade my upbringing for anyone else's. I loved it.

They threw great dinner parties in the 1980s. They drove up in BMWs, Porsches and other exotic cars, had colorful conversations and had unique perspectives on the world around them. They were on the rise enjoying life. It was the yuppie era and I was immersed in it.

I noticed the most successful people were spoken about in high regard when they weren't around, and they were respected by everyone.

I developed a love of many things that persist today. While I am passionate about fine automobiles and love to own and drive them, they do not define my identity. Instead they help remind me how fortunate I am in many ways. Just as those influential people modeled for me back then, I appreciate the person behind the wheel for their own story, what they've done to get there.

I have had plenty of friends that have come from humble means and weren't exposed to anything flashy at all in their lives. They gave me other sources of inspiration, such as having a sense of humor and an overall cool factor that was so authentic that I knew they were on to something big for their lives. It wasn't all about the money, but I did understand the value of it. Despite my mom's friendships and circles, she truly was a broke artist. I vividly recall a time when she received a $1,000 commission check for a piece of artwork. We felt like we'd just won the lottery, and I recall that feeling of appreciation and optimism for even more exposure and more checks in the future—even by me as a child.

When you experience the power of success, you start to look at the bigger picture—the next scene in your story.

That artwork was purchased by one of my mother's friends. I remember feeling great admiration for Michael Smith from the first day we met. I thought he was so cool and wanted to be like him back then (and even now).

Mike taught me that capitalism is a beautiful concept. He introduced me to sales with this guiding philosophy that I live by: The sky is the limit in sales, and attitude is everything.

Michael is self-made and witty. I remember the delicious and masterful comebacks flowed effortlessly from him at mom's dinner parties. He was often the butt of many 'short-man' jokes. One time a much taller friend of my mother's teased him that he wasn't sure how he saw over the dash of his brand-new BMW M6. Without missing a beat, Michael shot back with his charming British accent: "It's easy, John, I sit on my wallet." It was a great lesson to me. I was a short kid and I learned how I could keep things lighthearted, maintain my dignity and still get my message across. People are always going to come at you from many different angles for their own reasons, but you can clearly define your boundaries in a lighthearted way, and you don't have to engage them or take it personally. He wasn't the wealthiest guy in the room but he was the most confident and the one having the most fun. It didn't go unnoticed that his girlfriend, Melissa was the most attractive woman I had ever seen. I love them both to this day. Knowing what he has made of his life, and where he came from has been all I needed to succeed. I knew back then, as I do now, that the only thing that could stop me is me—and I never wanted that to happen.

Life is going to throw obstacles in your way. The people I most admire and appreciate are those who have found a way around those hurdles and rise to the top. Their stories are my inspiration. I hope one day my story will inspire others in the same way.

Neither being born into wealth, nor into poverty sets the level of what's possible in your life. Those things come from within. It's driven from the inside. If success is what you desire, look for the people and situations that give you the drive to go for it.

I've seen situations in my own family, where having wealth destroyed peoples' values and successes. It was actually a hindrance, and it all comes back to the qualities that exist inside that help you find success in a way that doesn't cut corners, but keeps you on the tried and true path—the system. My grandfather on my father's side was very wealthy, and for some of his children, my father included, it seemed to control them and be a source of misery. My uncle however, was the exception. He became another great inspiration in my life: He chose what he wanted to do and was so successful at it. He never forgot that life was worth living. He traveled, enjoyed good food and adventures, and created experiences in his life that were filled with goodness, not strife. It was in contrast to many others in his family. To this day, I try to drop everything whenever I can to go enjoy a beer with him and just listen. He's one of those people you can just be around and somehow feel that you're a better person because of it. It's awesome, and he's personally responsible for helping to instill three key uncompromising qualities into my life:

1. Modesty;
2. Honesty;
3. And, caring.

I consider these things to be gifts from my uncle. They are a pivotal part of who I try to be as a person and as a professional. They encompass everything I do—large or small. My Aunt Patricia is another big influence in my life because she is one of the strongest women I know. Through her examples and actions, I learned one of the most important things a real man can learn—to respect women and realize they are fully capable of being more powerful than any man could be. It is because of my aunt and those realizations that I can say with certainty; I am where I am today, on the verge of breaking out into something big...my biggest goal yet...because of the profound effects that women have had on my life.

THE SET-UP FOR SALES SUCCESS

You miss 100% of the shots
you don't take.

WAYNE GRETZKY

Selling cars at the Mercedes-Benz dealership was a sales job I seemed to have been working toward the entire time I grew up. With my previously mentioned passion for luxury cars, was there any better place to be? Little did I know, by being at the dealership and selling those beautiful cars, one of the best opportunities of my life would present itself to me.

One day, Marilyn Wilson, one of my clients at the dealership, came in to buy a new car. She was a breath of fresh air with her Los Angeles energy and style. What I loved most about Marilyn was her success. She was (and is) the most successful sales person in Ottawa's luxury home market. I appreciated having her as a client at the dealership, but what I really loved most about her was her passion and love for her career—and the high-level professional standards she set for herself.

What Marilyn did over time was suggest to me that with my sales excellence, I was capping myself by working in the luxury auto industry. There were only so many vehicles you could sell per month. And she expressed how she absolutely believed I could transfer my sales skills over to the real estate market and achieve more success. She had my attention, and eventually, I did listen.

I am a firm believer that if you want to succeed, you will not just dabble—you go all in and commit fully. So, I left my job in auto sales and ventured out, choosing high-end real estate as my target market. After all, Marilyn was a big influence. Why not learn from the ultimate master of the real estate game? I went to work for her, and an incredible new experience began that put all the disciplines I had developed to the test, along with new insights into what made for a great sales person that worked for clients—always.

Eventually I went out on my own and grew a team over the next decade and was consistently a top earner at my brokerage at the time. As often happens I came full circle and joined forces with Marilyn and had some of my best years. Since then I grew my stats and reputation even higher in the luxury market and raised my income level significantly. I had consistency as a high earner and realized quickly that a seven figure income was in my immediate future. All the tools were in place to grow my team even higher. With my good name tied to a well organized high-end global brand it was obvious Engel&Völkers was to become our new home and the sky was literally the limit. Their consistency in their high-end branding and global marketing was the perfect fit for our image.

It's a significant, important lesson to surround yourself with success in order to develop traits that successful people possess. You know, at this moment, I can almost hear what you're thinking. Sure, it's easy to have these massive months when you are working with luxury real estate. STOP! By thinking that way you are—regardless of your market—feeding your subconscious mind with garbage that will derail you before you can even begin. Your mindset and your practice of the *7 Figures to Success* will always trump the effect of the market.

> **I am in the trenches with all of you who are committed to sales excellence, which gives me raw and relevant information to help you. I'm reaching my goals, and it is due to the collective efforts of the *7 Figures*, which I hope will lead you to—you guessed it— 7 figures income.**

It is not as easy as everybody may believe to become a high-end real estate agent. If you want to be successful, your focus will never be geared towards a strategy of *fewer properties and higher commissions.* You'll want to have the same pipeline as someone who chooses to work in a $500K market, and you also have to network with the people who will eventually use your high-end real estate services, or gladly refer you to those who need your help. Who you surround yourself with becomes the essence of the results you get. And the kicker—it all has to be authentic!

You have to do difficult things and remain a well-intentioned person while doing them, to master your sales results. For example, I changed my circle of friends some years back, and by doing so it changed my life. I still love my old friends, but they did not lift me up or encourage me to succeed past a certain point. They wanted me to be "comfortable," and that is a step down for anyone who wants to excel in sales. Comfort equals stagnation, which equals a lack of passion for helping your clients. This is why today, I choose not to hang out with this particular group of buddies every weekend. We'll meet for a beer on occasion, and it's a good time.

They can see that money and success hasn't changed me, and now, I hope that through example, they can sense why they may have something to work toward for their own versions of success.

There are some who describe me as having a reasonable amount of charisma. Whatever it is, I do find people respond well to me in most situations. But I am not unique in that respect. There are plenty who make big money in my business and it boils down to their faithful use of a robust system. They know that one great month can never be an excuse to slack off.

THE 7 FIGURES TO SUCCESS SYSTEM

> Successful people do what unsuccessful
> people are not willing to do. Don't wish
> it were easier; wish you were better.
>
> JIM ROHN

Systems are the secret to maximizing your sustainable success in real estate. And, to state the obvious, a system isn't a system unless it is followed the same way—every day—systematically.

For a realtor (and anyone in sales), the key components to a successful system include the following features:

1. Personal outreach via notes and telephone calls;
2. Electronic outreach via emails;
3. Face-to-face touches with the right people to help you grow your business;
4. And, building a network of qualified potential clients and referral sources.

The word "qualified" is essential to all of this. You can have the longest list of people to send information to, but if you are sending it to someone who cannot use your services or is unwilling to refer you to others, then you are wasting your time with busy work. It may feel like you're following a system, but you're really not. You are the hamster on the wheel.

Building your network and keeping those within it in constant contact with you, knowing they already know and trust you, is a simple, satisfying, and brilliant way to build a career in real estate.

I know several agents who follow this to a T and consistently make huge money. The problem is most people follow the system until they get busy and then stop, which means they really are not always following a system. When you are committed to a system, it becomes as natural as breathing. You don't think, *Ugh. I don't feel like making those calls. I'll do it tomorrow.* You simply pick up the phone and make those calls.

I deliberately titled my system *7 Figures to Success* to inspire you, because that is exactly what the steps have done for me. By following them consistently they have helped me achieve and often surpass my goals. When you commit and follow this system and give it a full 365-day commitment, you will experience better success in your professional life. And those wins will also naturally carry over into your personal life. When you are successful, it feels good and shows through in all the ways you reveal yourself to others.

1. **Figure to be kind**
   Understanding kindness and what that really means to your career is an essential component of this system. You cannot have true success if you are not genuinely vested in the type of kindness that keeps you focused on ethical business that puts the clients' needs first. There is no corner-cutting. There is no faking kindness.

2. **Figure to ride the wave**

   Real estate goes in cycles, and when you interrupt your ride on the wave, you are sure to miss opportunities that will lead to the next one. Learn what you should do during these times, how to become a pro-wave rider, and how to stop the crash-and-burn at the end of the ride.

3. **Figure to be in it for the long haul**

   One word sums this up brilliantly—commitment! Full-on commitment brings long-term success. Every component required of you for being in real estate for the long haul will be covered in this chapter.

4. **Figure to surround yourself with greatness**

   If you want to skydive, you don't surround yourself with people afraid of heights. If you want to swim with sharks, you don't look for them in the local river. And if you want to achieve great things, you must surround yourself with the right people in all areas of your life.

5. **Figure to cut the BS**

   BSing yourself about where you are in your journey to success is a waste of mental energy and a sure way to feed your subconscious mind lousy thoughts and lies that cannot advance your cause. Identifying these behaviors and stopping them is pivotal for you to succeed in sales…not to mention overall happiness.

6. **Figure to find ways to overcome obstacles**

   Obstacles are a part of any person's journey to success. Without them, you would not have the opportunity to learn the lessons that help you grow stronger and better at what you do. There is a specific strategy involved in overcoming obstacles so they cannot hold you back or deter you for the long run.

7.   **Figure to send the elevator back down at some point**
     One of the hallmarks of success is remembering that there is someone
     else just beginning the journey. This means that as you move up in the
     world, you are well-served to give back to others. Use your expertise and
     experiences to mentor or coach someone else. So, send the elevator down
     and watch someone else begin to rise up!

Are you feeling the excitement?

Are you eager to learn about a system that will deliver something you
can see, experience, and feel in 365 days?

I am so grateful to share this with you, and I can't wait to see you succeed.
Let me know your story. You can reach out to me at chris@chrislacharity.com

Champions keep playing
until they get it right.

——————————

BILLIE JEAN KING

1

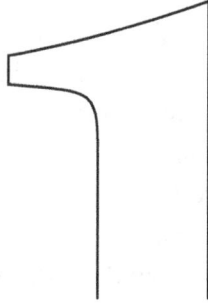

FIGURE TO BE KIND

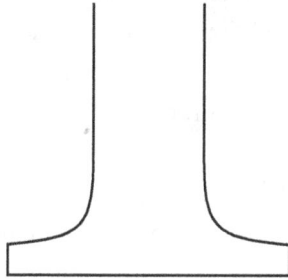

Kindness in words creates confidence.
Kindness in thinking creates profound-
ness. Kindness in giving creates love.

LAO TZU

I f you were to ask anyone, most would say they are kind. No one – that I've ever met, anyway – has ever said they do not want to be a kind person; that it's not their thing. But true kindness is easy to identify, both by intuition and by simply using your gifts of sight and sound.

I remember a guy I used to work with was thought of as the kindest, most thoughtful guy by many of his clients. He would smile at them, share great information, and talk in a way that had them leaving the dealership feeling like a million bucks. Then, once they were out the door, the opposite side of kindness showed through. His words were critical, mean-spirited, and showed no gratitude for the commission he'd just earned. That drove me crazy, because I knew he was faking it, and that it wasn't good for the environment at the dealership, any more than it was for him or those clients (even if they didn't fully realize it). There is no substitution for authentic kindness.

The definition of kindness:
kind-ness; /ˈkīn(d)nəs/ (n): the quality of being friendly, generous, and considerate.

We all have moments where we fail at being genuinely kind; it's human nature. However, those moments had best be the exception to the rule for 3 reasons:

1. **You never know who is watching and listening.**
   If you don't think a lack of kindness can come back and bite you in the butt, professionally and personally, you are inaccurate. It can. I've seen clients walk away from deals because they saw the unsavory side of their sales person (realtors and others).

2. **Focus on kindness is positive energy.**
   Lack of kindness is negative energy, and even if you have come across some person who may not deserve kindness, you can exercise silence instead of expressing your disapproval.

3. **You will be hindered in life when you are not kind.**
    People don't like to do business with negative people. Don't think you cannot be both kind and business-savvy at the same time. The two are very complementary traits, and it will never matter how your competition acts—how you act is what matters to your clients.

When kindness comes from within, it is something you cannot fake. It's genuine and authentic. What can top that?

THERE IS ALWAYS A REASON TO SMILE

In the car sales business, sales representatives come right up to you when you enter the showroom, or walk up to you when they see you pull into the outside lot to start looking at cars. There is nothing wrong with that, it is just the nature of the game. Everyone wants the lead.

In the luxury vehicle market, sales people don't usually do that. A customer will walk in and you'll look up and if they don't already have an appointment, they will decide to whom they wish to talk. I was fortunate to get to work with many of these walk-in clients. The number one reason for approaching me (that they shared) was that I was the only one with a smile.

A smile does great things for us internally, It releases feel-good neurotransmitters like dopamine, endorphins and serotonin making us a magnet for potential client sales. Some of these include:

1. Smiles are contagious—very few people can resist returning a genuine smile.
2. A smile makes you appear more friendly and approachable —being approachable isn't just some form of physical perception, It's also about exuding a friendly quality to another person. Some of the most beautiful people in the world exude this quality. It is natural and inviting to everyone.

3. A smile is life-enhancing—a bonus for anyone who has a desire to do great things and have amazing experiences in their life, for as long as they can!

Never discredit the impact of a smile. If you feel good, others feel good. It's one of the best techniques you can use to capture a potential client.

> Sometimes your joy is the source of your smile, but sometimes your smile can be the source of your joy.
>
> ――――――――――――
>
> THICH NHAT HANH

Take a moment to think of all the places where people are going to see your smile. They are endless, and include:

1. Through face-to-face interaction;
2. On your social media;
3. In your advertising;
4. Through observing you in person.

You cannot fake the message your smile gives towards others. Some people do have naturally grumpy expressions but are kind. If you are this type of person, be mindful of what you may look to be expressing, in contrast to what you are feeling. This brings me to another significant component of kindness: kindness in your written words.

KINDNESS IN WHAT YOU WRITE AND RELAY

It should be obvious if you are authentically kind, you do not go onto your social media accounts and air out every grievance you have about a situation or a specific individual. This type of behaviour could cost you your job. For a self-employed person (any person who relies on commissions to earn income) it will cost you potential clients, and perhaps an association with the type of brokerage firm that could take you to a higher level in your career and future goals if you're a realtor. You must be mindful and aware of your actions. Lack of attention and growth in those areas will likely cost you your career. I have certain political views but I never post them on social media. However tempting, it's a good way to lose clients quickly.

> **Separate personal social media life and your career. Not only will you look more professional, you will be more respected in your field.**

When it comes to how you communicate kindness in writing, as a realtor, you should focus on offering information and words that are appealing. Show a genuine intent for the recipient's wellbeing. Help them remember you as the kind realtor that doesn't just say you care—you do care. A thoughtful communication does wonders to express this. For you, this may include:

1. The emails you send out daily to remain in the forefront of past clients' or potential clients' minds;
2. The newsletters you create help bring meaning to your networking list—good information that lifts someone up and helps guide them to what may or may not be a great idea for them at any given time;
3. Letters in the mail—which still happen, although they are not as common;

4. Those handwritten notes that show kindness through special time and attention to write them. Hint: Don't be lazy, pen notes with your own hand. A note written by your assistant and signed by you loses most of its appeal. Make the effort count.

5. The words you use in your marketing efforts (if necessary). Not every realtor needs to invest expensive dollars into marketing after a certain point, because their system and network play key roles for self-promoting;

6. Any scripts you use with clients. I personally do not use scripts, as I feel more genuine and authentic when I just start from the heart and monitor my interactions as they progress. However, new realtors and others who are not as comfortable with that approach can benefit from learning a script until that type of message delivery becomes engrained in the subconscious mind.

There tend to be stigmas out there about sales people, in general, which suggests they could be focusing too much on the commission—nothing else. This isn't the case for many sales people, and they overcome those false perceptions by remembering that authentic kindness expressed through both the spoken and written word, and a genuine smile, reveals the true picture of their character.

MASSIVE RESULTS DON'T HAVE ROOM FOR MASSIVE EGOS

Ego trip: a journey to nowhere.

_____

ROBERT HALF

The ego is the arch nemesis to any realtor who cannot keep it in check. I've seen some really great people—individuals I considered to be very kind—make it big in their career and suddenly morph into this other person. Maybe that was the real version of them, the one lingering under the surface, but it was noticeable enough that it shocked me. And likely offended others.

Everyone has an ego. Being an egotist is detrimental to you as a person and as a professional. To most people, experiencing egotistical behavior is similar to a smoke and mirrors effect—it's an illusion to give someone misdirection about who they really are. Over time, it becomes a challenging façade to keep up and others will begin associating it with one of two things: 1) a lack of confidence and healthy self-esteem; 2) the egocentric person is purporting to be greater than their results reveal them to be. Neither of these are good—and certainly cannot last indefinitely.

I freely admit when I was younger my ego got the best of me a time or two, and I also saw egotistic qualities in some of the people I hung around with—and even dated. It never felt or settled quite right. I just knew something was missing. I've come to realize, what was missing was their authentic self—a confident self that felt assured about who they were and what they could offer. As it turns out, there is no need for the illusion of success, because it cannot beat the real deal.

A big risk you take by clinging to your ego is you are going to increase volatile situations in your day and reduce meaningful, pro-growth opportunities for your career.

Have you ever had a fight with someone who kept arguing with you even though you knew what you were saying was correct? They said what they had to say, you countered with what you had to say. It went on and on, escalating with each exchange. Then BAM! You're now in a heated situation. Who's to blame? The answer is—both of you.

It is okay to disengage from a tense situation, even when you are right, because once you close down all reasoning and discussion, you've both effectively lost the argument. It's pointless, and it's not a quality that a genuinely kind person can possess. It's absolutely okay to look at that person and speak bluntly, "This conversation is out of control so I'm just going to walk away." Then—and this is key—walk away. If you are someone who enjoys that feeling of having the last word, this will help you do that without giving up more dignity or empowering your ego even further. This is good information to know!

There are lessons to learn from egotistical-inspired mistakes. I am personally grateful to have experienced them in my life. You've got to let that ego go, and here are 5 ways you can begin to do that:

1. **Let go, forgive, and move on**
    When people hold onto things that have happened to them long after they have run their course, it usually indicates that "baggage" has impacted them in some significant way. Maybe it's a relationship—*she broke up with me, but I knew she wasn't good enough for me.* Professionally, it can be that client you felt a really great rapport with suddenly goes with a different realtor—and to add salt to the wound, the "new realtor" is a friend of a friend who is new to the business. You have to let these things go, because living in those past moments without learning from them will stop your growth today. Make no mistake about it, today is what matters. Today is the day that is relevant to your success.

2. **Be honest and forthright**
    This is twofold: you have to be honest with yourself and honest with those you serve. Both are necessary. If you put energy into lying to yourself, where does the line of truth present itself? This line is necessary, as it will allow you to best assist your clients. They are entrusting you with a lot—so a lot you must give. (Does that sound like Yoda? Hey…he's wise.)

3. **Surrender your "control freak" tendencies**
    When you think you have to control everything around you, you are really saying that if some element does not go your way, you're toast.

Work with what you can, use a system to pay attention to what you must, and realize you can gain the know-how to address any surprise that is thrown at you and stop it from making you become off-kilter. In fact, if you're disciplined and solution-oriented in a time of crisis with a client, you will be the professional that stands out in that moment and you'll be remembered. (Hint: breathe!)

4. **Be kind to yourself**

It is unnecessary to beat yourself up just as it is foolish to build yourself up falsely. You are human and even if you become the super-agent of the 21st century, you will still be human. This means mistakes, lessons, triumphs, and humility are a part of your experience. Embrace this...and remember your goodness to yourself is a direct reflection of how you can be good for others too.

5. **Be grateful for what you currently have**

It's easy to think about your next big commission—the home that is supposed to close in 60 days, for example. Of course, you're grateful for that, but in reality, a deal isn't a deal until it's closed. When you wake up each day you should be grateful you have an opportunity to use your system to create connections that will help other peoples' needs be met while you also fulfill yours. That's just one example. Personally, I think it's excellent to be grateful for just about everything you touch (IF you surround yourself with the right things).

These 5 simple tips are ones most of us know at a base level, but easily lose sight of in our busy, chaotic lives. Kindness will always trump anything that isn't considered kind. You have to have the faith and confidence it will play out that way. Fighting it will get you into trouble—maybe not legal trouble, but trouble with your goal of sales success.

You must train yourself to do what is right, because there is never an excuse for being disrespectful to a client or a peer. If you are, quite honestly, you do not deserve that deal. And furthermore, you will have no way of knowing what additional deals you have lost either.

FIGURE TO DO THESE 3 THINGS

Nothing can beat being authentically kind from your heart. Always serve your clients' best interests above your own. You can always do things in a better way and improve your presentation to others so that your kindness—which cannot be faked for long—shines through. You are in charge of your own effectiveness here.

1. **Understand the Universal Rule of all-things-real-estate: It is not about you!**

   As realtors, we often think everything is about us. What we need; what we want; what we can do. This really isn't true, and it's a sign of egotism. You may not feel this describes you, but starting today, consciously remind yourself not to act on your personal emotions. This is still a business, and while it is an emotion-laden business for clients, you are the one who is supposed to keep the voice of reason to help your clients every step of the way. *Everything you do is meant to represent your client's best interests.* Even if you have a dilemma, you need to think of it from only one perspective: what is best for your client. There are no exceptions to this rule.

2. **Take the emotion out of your actions in business.**

   This is one of our biggest responsibilities as a realtor. We should be the mediator that removes emotion from emotional situations for buyers and sellers. Don't squabble over a thousand dollars on a $2M deal because it looks unprofessional. It doesn't serve the best interest of your client who is likely to spend far more than that by having their house on the market for even one additional month.

3. **Learn your lessons the first time.**
When you learn a lesson the first time around it can be a positive, supporting moment, which helps you realize the importance of kindness in your work. However, if you are so thick-skulled you keep repeating the same mistakes, you can rest assured you are not being kind to your clients. You are denying them the opportunity to get the best and most feasible deal. And, over time, that will come back to haunt you. Your first indicator will be a zero-referral stream, or referrals that are some of the most challenging deals you can imagine (thereby sucking you more deeply into even rougher lessons).

Kindness will always matter because it makes all peoples' lives better. As a realtor (or any sales professional), you can do a great deal to bring the power of kindness to the forefront of your community's mind via all your gestures, actions, and most importantly, your attitude toward it. If you want to contribute to something great, contribute kindness to your profession. I'd love to hear your story of kindness in your career. Please share it with me on my Facebook page at Chris Lacharity.

> Guard well within yourself that treasure, kindness. Know how to give without hesitation, how to lose without regret, how to acquire without meanness.
>
> GEORGE SAND

2

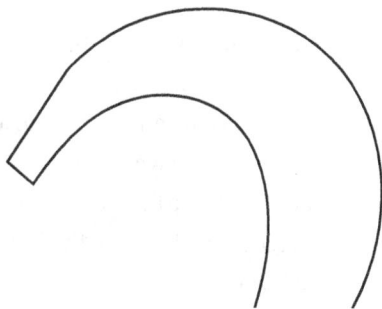

FIGURE TO RIDE THE WAVE

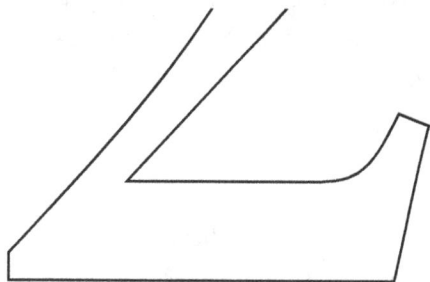

There's no room to make excuses and not take action when you want to succeed in real estate. You need to find a way to be there when opportunity does strike.

CHRIS LACHARITY

M any businesses are cyclical and that brings about one of the ugliest words that people can face—uncertainty. Real estate is most always termed as cyclical. Does that mean you have to accept there will be slow times? Absolutely not! I have made it so I never have a slow time, and my December and January can be just as busy as any other time of the year. I will not even allow myself to recognize slow months. Why? Because there is always something you can do to grow your business. With diligent attention, you'll be amazed at the results you get.

A wave can come along at any given time and it will also dissipate without notice, but when you are committed to taking care of your pond (your market), there will always be a new one coming. You just have to keep your eyes open and commit to doing what is necessary all of the time.

No excuses.

No complaints.

No assumptions.

Be grateful for the opportunities you have—when you receive them—and allow them to energize you. You should never have a day when you receive a referral from someone and it is not an opportunity you are stoked to receive. This is possible to do in an authentic way when you understand the reasons why you chose to do what you are doing for your career.

THE "PROVIDING FOR" MINDSET

Service is the rent we pay for being. It is the very purpose of life, and not something you do in your spare time.

MARIAN WRIGHT EDELMAN

We all have different ways in which we receive our motivation to work harder and smarter so that we can experience success. In some countries, the motivation is the expectations that stem from your family. For example, if you are the oldest son, it may be expected that you will financially provide for your parents' wellbeing when they get older. Or, if you are the youngest daughter, you may be expected to be the one to take care of your parents' needs when they are no longer able to do that for themselves.

For those of us who have grown up in North America, we're not as likely to view our responsibilities in the same way. Many never consider the thought of taking care of their parent(s), especially if the parents are financially well-off.

Are you wondering why I'm even bringing this up? The reason is simple—within your choices to succeed you should think of a bigger picture than just "you," the individual. Your decisions in your professional life can lead to an incredible opportunity to positively affect those you care about. And while I'm a firm believer that everyone should accomplish their own goals, I also believe that you do owe something back to those people who have helped make you successful. For me, this does include my parents—my mom, in particular.

Through having the mindset I want to, and I am willing and able to, emotionally or financially provide something for my mom, I have found one of the most exceptional rewards of my hard work. All the time, energy, and drive are undoubtedly worth it. In fact, it means more because it has value that goes beyond a paycheck. Not so strangely, this belief has also led to better paychecks.

Think about your life and what brings value to it? Go beyond the money and ask yourself:

1. What ways could my financial gains help someone else?
2. Are there any charities or organizations that could benefit from me using my skills and talents in real estate to my fullest potential?
3. Who has helped and supported me, making me who I am today?

Asking yourself these types of questions is an inspiring way to recognize all the reasons you have to ride the wave for as long as you can (when one comes your way). The time will come when it fades away and there is nothing but a ripple in the water. Where you are at the moment defines you at that place in time.

NEVER JUMP OFF A MOVING WAVE

I cannot tell you how many times I've come across realtors who are so excited because they've just closed a "big deal", or they've had a string of listings come their way. They feel amped up and excited—as they should—but seem to forget a few key points that will always remain vitally important to their success:

1. **No deal is a closed deal until the paperwork is signed and a commission check is in hand.**
    Never count a deal as closed and completed before it is closed and completed. Even if it is the morning of closing, don't move on to what you want to do with your commission until you actually receive that check. Experienced (and grounded) realtors recognize that the unexpected can surface on the day of a real estate closing. Bad weather could delay the relocating buyer from getting into town; the bank may have a last minute glitch with the funding; a circumstance can just change; a pipe may burst the night before closing... You just never know what could happen, and while you should never operate in a "worst case scenario" mode, you shouldn't operate in a way that assumes all will happen the way you plan, simply because you want it to. Keeping a level head is something you can develop and grow grateful for (and not drive yourself crazy).

2. **Many opportunities come in waves.**
    Imagine this scenario...

You just landed a really sweet deal and you are itching for a vacation. You decide to book that trip to some place warm and inviting (it's the middle of winter, after all) and you're set to leave three days after that home closes. You're excited and you're preparing, and then the phone starts ringing. Someone wants to see your latest listing. Another person would like to meet with you next week when they are in town. One of your favorite past clients has an urgent referral for you. But, where are you? You're mentally checked out and on vacation.

It's almost like an unexplained part of the Law of Attraction—when you fully invest your thoughts into a situation other than work that you're excited about, work will start coming your way. What do you do when that happens? You can either:

1. Bring in a recruit to help you out (one the customer will begin to build rapport with);
2. Hope that the client can wait until you are home;
3. Or, lose the lead because your vacation doesn't jive with their needs.

Please don't get me wrong. I'm not saying you can never take a vacation or some time off to recharge if you need it, but you should be smart about how you go about doing so. If your business is in a high tide, keep on moving along, because you'll earn valuable clients, income, and the opportunity for your vacation will still exist.

3. **Don't talk yourself into your own busy seasons.**
I am a firm believer that if you make assumptions you are going to be slow during certain months—just because other realtors have said they always are—you are only assuring yourself of one thing: you are going to be slow during those months. I challenge you to flip your perspective.

Accept that when others in your business say that they are going to be slow during certain months, they are really giving you the opportunity to *not* be slow. For me, I never lower my sales goals because of other peoples' stated trends. My goals are as big and aggressive as I want them to be, regardless of the time of year. In fact, when writing this book, I had the biggest January of my career—one that surpassed my goals.

Regardless of how long you've been in real estate, it is never too late to revamp how you think about the waves of business that come your way. You may be confident you can turn some deals away for that desired vacation and still be fine—and that is great—but the time may come when those deals don't come so easily any longer, and if you haven't planned right, you may not have any idea of what to do next. Waves are not infinite.

THE RIPPLE EFFECT OF A SINGLE COMMISSION

When you look at an ocean, there isn't just one wave at a time in motion. There are a series of things happening. Some of which are on the rise, some have reached a plateau, and others have started to fall. The same is true of your business, which is what makes it ever-evolving and constantly shifting.

———————————

CHRIS LACHARITY

We all need to earn our commissions in order to make a living and manage our lives financially. This is logical and I'd never suggest someone work for free; however, I would suggest you look beyond what a single paycheck brings you and see the larger picture. Your goal should never be to close a deal with a client, never to hear from them again. You either want their next deal (whether it's buying or selling), or you would like them to refer you to their friends because of what you did to help them.

I once listed a drafty old stone mansion for sale that needed a big renovation. I was the seller's rep for this transaction and that seller happened to be a country (this mansion was their embassy). The asking price they requested was high for this place, especially considering the work that needed to be done. They were asking $1.79M, and with that price, we'd only been able to get one couple to walk through the door and consider the property.

He was a hard-working professional and obviously did quite well for himself, and his wife was charming and gorgeous. They were basically an "it" couple, clearly surrounded by the finest of things life had to offer—including the hottest, newest high-end SUV on the market at the time. They arrived for the showing with their own agents—a couple's team.

When you're representing the seller, you can't have a lot of interaction with the buyers directly, only their agent(s). So, I watched this couple and I saw they were clearly intrigued by the house and did recognize its value—much more so than the agents. However, you could tell this deal was potentially huge for them—one that would have been monumental in their career. They visited the mansion, and then wanted to come a few more times. The agents representing the buyers began to stop coming to the appointments, seeing that everything was all under control, and there I was, now the one answering these questions for the buyer. (It's important to note that I didn't encourage this to happen, as it could be deemed unethical by some, especially if a buyer's representation agreement was signed. However, there was no such agreement and in time, the agents were not there.)

I found the other agents' behavior odd, and it presented me with a big opportunity. Eventually, I convinced the buyer to put in an offer at any price they felt fair and I would do my best to get them a great deal. They put in an offer of $1.3M on the $1.79M listing.

Most agents will quickly kill a "lowball offer" on a property immediately, but it is important to not be "most agents" if you want to be successful. You have to take advantage of any leads that exist and play the deal through until it either closes or dies.

With the offer in hand, I made a call to the seller's representative, who lived abroad and also had the decision-making authority for the deal. He'd never been to Canada but did claim to have knowledge regarding the "world" of real estate. I presented him the low offer of $1.3M and his response was to "forget about it," and "keep doing what I was doing." He wanted someone more serious, and this is where I had to have a serious and real conversation. I responded with some facts:

1. No one, aside from this couple, were serious enough to walk through the door.
2. No one, aside from this couple, had even considered putting an offer in.

I suggested the gentleman at least counteroffer, but he wouldn't. He was persistent. When I had a chance, I shared this story with the owner of my brokerage, who, at the time, had become like a father to me with all of his great advice. He suggested I hop on a plane and visit the decision-maker to discuss the deal face-to-face. It was an interesting idea and I had a few things to consider. It was a 25-hour flight, for starters. I didn't take that flight but instead, I pleaded my case over the phone and achieved a counter-offer with a $100K reduction.

From there, we went back and forth. I kept pushing, grinding and doing whatever I could do to keep the deal moving forward. And finally, a price was agreed upon—$1.7M. The effort had worked and more so, the clients shared how hard I worked for them with others. This all happened from talking with people who think creatively and being committed to the only serious clients who had looked at the home. I didn't read how to do this in a book; I was attuned to the wave of one potential buyer and took note of the passion and emotion that was a part of the process, from both the buyer's and seller's sides. This is one reason why I absolutely love high-end real estate!

Most sellers' reactions to a low-ball offer are going to be negative and dismissive initially. Their emotions may tell them they should be offended and then resist a counter-offer—which costs nothing to put out there. Right now, I am going through this exact same thing with one of my listings. We have just received our only offer since listing the property and the seller wants to ignore it. As an agent, you have to get your sellers to understand the full scope of an offer, emotions aside. There is a very real chance this could be the scenario (as it has proven itself true, many times):

Oftentimes, your first offer is your best offer; if you turn your back on it and it goes away, you have a good chance of finding yourself wishing you had it back, once you realize no new offers are coming.

Don't be afraid to have these real conversations with your sellers, because you are there to represent them. You can't force them to consider anything, but you can give your professional advice. "Okay, so this person is $109K off your asking price, yes, but they are also the most committed buyer on the planet right now." Counter-offer!

Observation shows a typical response from a seller has a fairly consistent pattern. The seller could come down $30K and then the buyer counters by coming up $20K. Now you're $59K apart—an already substantial shrink in the gap. Most times, the seller will then mirror what just happened, and before you know it, the gap is $39K apart. The buyer follows the pattern and mirrors the counter as well. $19K apart—split the difference and you get a deal, and both parties feel good! This is how negotiating works and your clients will usually follow your lead. So be calm, be precise, and stay focused on the details.

One of the things I love most about residential real estate is the emotions involved in it. They are reminders you are dealing with real people and their dreams, needs, and hopes. You can't find that kind of spark in commercial real estate (at least I don't). My role is to help make everyone happy and use all the emotions swirling around to craft a deal that is acceptable to both parties. You cannot beat this feeling!

Buyers and sellers want to work with realtors who get the job done!

Your *wave* is going to be dependent on your ability to negotiate a deal comfortably and to look beyond what may seem insulting, and into what is actually possible to do. To do this:

1. Never assume you know the buyer's mind.
2. Never assume you know the seller's mind.
3. Never assume an answer.

Making assumptions is never good. It seldom reaps the long-term rewards that come with a wave of deals from people who trust you can get the job done for someone else the way you did for them!

STANDING OUT IN THE SEA OF REALTORS

Remember, 50% of your real estate
career is simply meeting the demands of
someone—they either want to buy or sell
a home—and the other 50% is what you
bring to the deal to make you the stand-out
realtor and the option clients want.

CHRIS LACHARITY

News flash: realtors often get thrown into the same category as used car salesmen. They are often thought of as untrustworthy and considered shifty. This is what you can be up against in this profession, which is why you have to be genuine. Let clients know you are there for them through thick and thin, honestly and earnestly. You should be having real conversations with the people you meet to address their emotions and the logistics of the business they have to conduct whether buying or selling. You must have all of these components covered in order to be successful in residential real estate. Knowing this is one of my greatest assets, and people share with me that I'm trustworthy because of this.

Now is a good time to remind you that you can be perfectly trustworthy, but give the misperception that you are not. Working on relaying that trustworthiness, becomes the next important step (if this is your obstacle). To do this, you'll find results if you:

- **Remember that a deal is not about you**
  Many agents have never discovered that the deal is not about them, or they struggle to put their ego aside. Stop talking about yourself and start

talking with your client about what they need. Real estate clients are very in tune to which realtors appear to be in it primarily for their own interests.

- **Let clients know your best interest is their best interest**
State your intention: that getting your client the best deal for the house they are buying or the home they are selling is your desire. Again, it's about them!

- **Share how you are in it for the long haul**
Clients strongly resist agents who appear to just want a commission and nothing else. You have to find tactful ways to share this isn't the case with clients. Let them know a $10 - $20K difference in price is minimal for your paycheque. This assures them your primary concern is for them. Their thoughts the transaction was successful and their happiness with the outcome is what defines your success!

Even when you take steps to do the right thing by your clients, you may occasionally meet resistance, and you should expect that. I once sold a guy's house who had previously fired me. I was honest and forthright with him when I brought a buyer to the table and revealed the highest amount of money he'd get for the house. By this time, he believed me, but confessed he couldn't afford to pay any commission if he took the offer. Since I was representing the buyers and this was the house they wanted, I still put the deal together, because that was the right thing to do. I signed a waiver that my commission was off the table if there was no money left over, and if there was, that would be my payment. There was no money left for me at the end of the transaction (and I sustained a $50K loss); however, there was something more valuable for me to continue riding the wave.

1. This client came back to me for his real estate deals in the future, some of which I received a double-ended commission because I represented both the buyer and the seller ($120K gained).

2. This client continued to send me referrals.
3. I received credit for a $2M sale, which was excellent for my sales statistics—which can mean as much as the money.

All of this shows the benefits of the Law of Reciprocation. When you do something to honour an agreement and to help another person, this will come back to you. You don't do it expecting it to come back, but when you do these things with an attitude and heart for service, surprising and wonderful things naturally happen. It's incredible, actually. This type of response also leads to an ocean full of waves you can keep riding for quite a long while.

FIGURE TO DO THESE 3 THINGS

Create your own dynamic impact in your body of water—your market—so you are the one who creates the waves, then hop aboard them, and ride them out until the end.

1. **Create and follow a system.**
    If you don't have a system, create one. I have been inspired and benefited from the Brian Buffini system. It is an excellent base for what I do in my real estate practice, and it has given me a solid foundation for creating a system that ensures I remain mindful when I:

    1. Make the calls I should make daily;
    2. Send the emails required by me every day;
    3. Write notes to past, present, and potential clients;

    The key to making your system work for you is to ensure you don't fall into that excuse of "I'm too busy." Calls and emails are probably a fifteen-minute commitment, so don't treat them like they are an all-day event. I always do my system follow-ups in the morning.

It's worth noting that when people get ready to go on vacations they start to use a system (although sometimes unwittingly). They call people to give them a heads-up. In doing so, they put themselves into the forefront of clients' minds. It opens up opportunities for referrals and new business. Imagine how well it would work for you if you treated every day like it was vacation-preparation day. I am confident that you could increase your business substantially if you had this type of energy and discipline.

2. **Find a way to use all 7 Figures to Success until they become habit.**
    The 7 Figures to Success is not just a system. It is a way to approach both your personal and professional life. The *Figures* help you focus your efforts on being an ethical, inspired, and service-minded realtor. They will lead you to become a prominent professional in your career for your market, as well as a person who contributes to your community at large. The waves will help you rein in consistent results that will help you master this.

3. **Remember, do not bring your ego to the table.**
    If you are in a situation where you really need money and it's hard to imagine putting in any amount of work for no return, keep in mind you have to look beyond your current situation and into the situation you are striving to be in. There have been times over the course of my career when I needed money pretty badly and wanted to abandon my disciplines and system. My ego was bruised and I felt disrespected but I managed to find ways to set these feelings aside because they served no greater purpose for me. They will not for you, either. Do I still struggle on occasion with thoughts like this? I do at times, but it is quite rare because I believe in the benefits of not bringing ego and insecurities to the table. It has paid off through earning more business, better business, and now I have a desired reputation for being a go-to realtor in the luxury real estate market.

Whatever you believe with
feeling becomes your reality.

———————

BRIAN TRACY

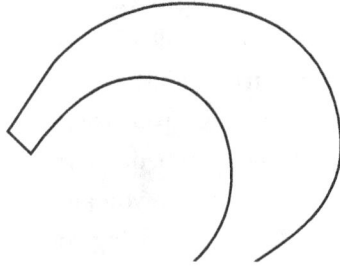

3
FIGURE TO BE "IN IT" FOR THE LONG HAUL

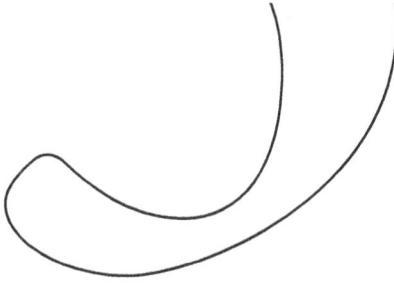

When you are a realtor it's different to being a CEO, who will get paid no matter what. You have to commit to the long haul for your career so you can set it up to have those steady paycheques coming in. No one else is going to do this for you.

CHRIS LACHARITY

A re you someone who is dabbling in real estate to see if you like it or will be successful at it before you go "all in?" This is a common approach for many people interested in the industry.

The sheer number of realtors can also overwhelm some people who don't have the confidence, developed system, or referral base to start benefitting from. If this sounds like you—or someone you know—know this: you have to stop dabbling and commit to real estate being your main livelihood if you want to really excel at it financially. Not only is this mindset good for you, it's also better for your clients.

Think about this…

You're at your grandmother's house for a great holiday meal. She mentions to you that her neighbours' grandson just started a career in investment banking and she thinks you should give him a chance—allow him to prove himself.

You're listening to Grandma, but thinking, I'm not about to hand over a large sum of money to a new guy just to give him the chance to prove himself. My experienced investment banker is quite brilliant already. I don't want to! Would you let Grandma persuade you? Probably not!

Why is it so easy for people to recommend that you use an inexperienced real estate agent to give them their first deal? It happens a lot. Some of the reasons may be:

1.   They just want to help somebody succeed;
2.   They don't understand the value and intricacies that are a part of real estate transactions;
3.   They want you to do it so they don't feel they have to (yes, that's possible);
4.   Or, they assume that just because someone took a few months of real estate school they are extremely qualified.

Yes, people have to get their start somewhere, but it shouldn't come at the cost of your best interests—ever. At the very least, a newer agent should have a few things in place that can give you some assurances if you're the customer. And if you are reading this as the new realtor, you should consider getting these things in place:

1. Mentors;
2. Continuing education;
3. Opportunities to watch the pros in progress as they make deals happen;
4. Work under an experienced lead agent who gets involved and teaches you from their experience.

I am always glad to have anyone who wishes to shadow me to see how the entire process of a real estate deal is conducted—starting with rapport with client and all the way through the paperwork, etc. A few take advantage of the opportunity to learn and grow in this way but overall, not many are committed to shadowing.

You can be likeable, kind, and have the sweetest grandmother in the world, but that doesn't mean that someone owes you the opportunity to work on their real estate transaction. You have to earn it.

There is no better way to gain the experience, success, and results that a client who trusts you with their real estate transaction deserves than being in it for the long haul.

IT'S EITHER "I DO" OR "I DON'T"

We are what we repeatedly do. Excellence then, is not an act, it is a habit.

ARISTOTLE

Real estate is a business where paperwork, laws, and market trends can change rapidly, in all types of markets from high- to low-end. There can be a sudden market drop or increase based on some economic factor that realtors certainly have no control over. A new marketing strategy may take off that helps bring focus to homes in a new way (such as the "talking home"), but guess what? No matter what happens in the world around you that can shift the real estate market, the one thing that cannot be eliminated is the need for you. Houses do not show themselves, computers don't manage human emotions, and contracts do not get magically drafted. Real people—hopefully experts—do this work. If you are not going to commit fully with an "I do" to real estate, you are not needed. In reality, you're not likely to close many deals, either. You're more likely to sit in on open houses or take a small cut from an experienced realtor to help with their work load.

So, ask yourself: "Do you or don't you want to be a successful realtor?" If you do, then have the confidence to go into it full-time. Debate these questions:

- **What do you feel you may get out of your career?**
  If a five or six figure paycheck for a single closing is your number one answer, you may face challenges. It's not impossible to do, but money is never the real motivator for anyone when it comes down to true mastery and satisfaction in a career.

- **How will you be available to show homes to potential clients when it works for them if you have other commitments that take up your time?**

  It would be tacky and ineffective to try to book out showing a home during your lunch hour from another job, for an example. Not only could the client who wants to see the house be running late, but they may be excited and have a lot of questions and be ready for action. You don't want to cut momentum off if you can keep it going by putting together an offer to purchase.

- **What amount of time does it take to become efficient and a master in all aspects of real estate transactions?**

  Trick question! It's hard to ever become this master. While there are some people that are as "all-knowing" as you can get, it has taken them many years of studying, planning, and actually doing real estate. The best teacher for real estate mastery is conducting transactions, not reading about them. Continuing education to become better is important, but action is what's truly required.

- **How do you define your value?**

  If you believe working for a discount broker is the way to get more deals, you are still going to experience clients who don't feel you're worth the commission. The one thing that's impossible is to talk a potential client into why you have value. You must demonstrate it, and showing you're willing to market yourself as a "discount" only discounts one thing—your skills, expertise, and abilities. People don't expect to buy a market-entry car and get the same level of service as you would with a high-end Mercedes.

- **What are your thoughts about selling?**

  You don't have to be a born salesperson to sell real estate, but you do have to know how to sell. Part of the art of selling, is explained wonderfully by Tom Hopkins. He is referring to financial services, but these same things do hold true for real estate, as well. He says: *"Mastering the art of selling involves mastering the craft of providing your clients the education, products, services, and personal contact before, during and after the sale that they want, need and, more important, deserve. That's how you succeed. That's how you'll not only survive and grow in this business, but will thrive, prosper, and achieve greatness through it."*

Through these questions, you can have a meaningful thought process and discussion about it if you have what it takes to be in it for the long haul. You have to think long-term, or else you're not thinking it through with the due diligence the decision requires—and your future clients deserve.

> **You may be able to hit a home run in the beginning and make a fast buck, but you want sustainable bucks. Being in it for the long haul helps to build sustainability.**

Yes, there are those who feel a good deal is where everyone loses or just one person gains. That's crap to me. A good deal is a fair deal and everybody wins. I'm not saying I haven't done some great deals where my client really capitalized on a situation; I have, but that was my job. I represented that one side of a transaction that looked to me to get them the best deal possible. I am a ruthless warrior, but I know there are lines you do not cross. I would never jeopardize someone's wellbeing or put someone in an unsafe position just to get a deal. It's an easy choice to make, not only morally, but because I choose to be in this career for the long haul. That means I am responsible for the decisions I make and their impact on the lives of everyone involved with them.

So, as you look at your career right now, ask yourself if you are ready to say, "I do" or "I don't."

THE FEAR OF BEING PHASED OUT

Changes always take place in the real estate world that cause realtors to panic and fear they're soon going to be obsolete. This makes the thought of committing to just real estate alone a decision that seems unwise, because what if one day it all changes. Poof! You're no longer needed.

This type of knee-jerk reaction is both contagious and distracting. At the last brokerage I was at, I walked in on a meeting that was taking place right in front of my office door. They were all in heavy discussion, yelling about the Competition Bureau—the independent Canadian law enforcement agency that ensures that businesses operate in a competitive manner—and their latest announcement. Now, individuals who were going to sell their home on their own would be able to list it on the MLS (Multiple Listing Service).

So, my boss stopped me and asked me what I thought about it. He asked me to address everyone. After I was filled in, I said, "What better vehicle to get listings than this. You can call these people and say that you noticed their house isn't selling; maybe it's time for them to use an agent. Before this, we didn't have that ability because we didn't have the information." Half of the room saw I was right, and the other half resisted.

It's natural we want to feel relevant and needed in our work. With real estate, we can always feel that way when we put in the time to follow our system and build up our successes.

The truth is, some agencies or government entities are always going to be stepping in and trying to change something or another in real estate. At times, it's a response to poor practices and at other times, the changes are good ideas. In the end, only you can ensure and maintain your confidence and strategies through the changes. They are hardly ever earth-shattering—unless you build them up to be.

So, my advice to everyone is to "stay calm and have a back-up plan."

Even I have a back-up plan and I'm still in hot pursuit of all my exciting goals. I am creating a CRM (Customer Relationship Management) system that works for realtors and helps others through coaching services that help them organize and do what I do every day. The beauty of the system I am finessing is that it is highly relevant, as I am still in the process of refining it by using it and seeing how it generates results that work for my goals. And when it works for me, it will be a repeatable process that will work for other realtors, or even sales professionals who rely on relationship-building, at large.

There is nothing wrong with having a plan as long as it doesn't slip into first position and become your primary plan (unless you want it to be). When you have a job to do, you have to put in work to do it exceptionally well. Lackluster self-standards lead to results that make your fears of being phased out a self-fulfilling prophecy. But work hard and your commitment to your craft will open doors and create connections. This is by far the easiest way to accomplish the successes that you are figuring out for your career.

A MARK OF EXCELLENCE

When you have the opportunity to go face-to-face with a potential client, it is completely in your hands to deliver the dynamic presentation followed by honest and forthright information that will earn you the opportunity.

CHRIS LACHARITY

People who are only half-vested in their careers are seldom excellent at presenting—an important part of a realtor's job. Posture, mannerisms, and confidence in your tone lack when you have a poor presentation. When this happens, that client has no reason to assume you are the best, most qualified person to help them. You must show your value, and if you can't, you will struggle.

I've seen presentations from agents that look like it's their first one ever, and they've been in the business for five years. Likewise, I've seen presentations from a new agent that make it look like they're in charge and you have no reason to doubt their abilities at all. Of course, it all comes down to what you do after you get the contract, because a deal isn't a deal until it's completely closed. However, if you can't even get a deal to reach that point, you may have a problem and even if you say you're in it for the long haul, you aren't showing that will be the case. It ultimately comes down to action over words.

Some people will tell you that you need PowerPoints, charts, and all sorts of gadgets to make your presentation pop, but I would have to disagree. You have to do what works for you and it's very seldom those gadgets work for realtors. People are at their best when they are connecting with their audience. It's hard to do that when you're staring at a PowerPoint, fumbling with the computer buttons in hopes that it'll stay working, etc. Looking at someone in the eye sharing your experience and knowledge is certainly a more effective strategy.

I have built my business up by being comfortable with who I am, which means that I have no canned presentations that I bring to the conversation with a potential client. I have information and data on their property (if it's a listing) and then I go from there. My presentation is natural, passionate, and effective because it reveals my expertise, true thoughts, and personality.

I share stories that relate to my clients and you should consider doing that too. It'll take you farther in all areas of your career when you do this. The confidence and position this guides you toward is highly beneficial in giving clients comfort in sending you referrals. They want others to see for themselves what they now see in you.

What I'm really emphasizing is don't fool yourself! It's easier to do than you may realize.

I recall a time when I first started in real estate when someone in the business I really admired (and still do), Rob Marland, asked me a question: "Chris, are you 100% committed?" I'll be honest, I thought it was a bit of a jerk move to ask me that, and I snapped back: "I'm here, aren't I?"

Rob didn't say anything further and it wasn't until years later that the meaning of that question hit me. I was talking the talk, but not walking the walk. I definitely was not acting like I was in it for the long haul.

When you are committed for the long haul you can answer "yes" emphatically to any of these questions:

1. Do my actions show I am 100% committed to my goals? YES!
2. Am I committed to the numbers I set for myself each and every day? YES!
3. Am I motivated by my career? YES!
4. Do I refuse to let anything hold me back? YES!
5. Is this where I'm meant to be? YES!

If it's "yes," then the action is the result of your convictions. You'll do enough to grow in your career and no one will ever speculate that you just "dabble in real estate." They'll know you are a focused and committed professional, and someone that won't just disappear or fade away. That's a pretty awesome place to be.

3 WAYS TO SHOW YOU'RE IN IT FOR THE LONG HAUL

The journey of a thousand miles begins with one step.

————

LAO TZU

The very actions of someone who is in real estate for the long haul show a distinction between them and the dabblers in real estate—and there are plenty of those to create the contrast. Sure, there'll be exceptions now and again, but overall, a realtor does have focus on all areas of their business. They build up their value in different ways, take care of their existing client's needs, as well as highlight why a future client should choose them.

These three considerations are a great way to distinguish yourself as a serious real estate professional.

1. **Take less commission in certain situations.**
   One area with various shades of "grey" is that of commission. When you discount yourself via your paycheque, you're discounting your value to your clients. However, there can be times when it is very logical to take a lesser commission in exchange for something of benefit to you and your career goals. For example, when I took zero commission on that large deal, my sales stats showed I'd closed a high-end deal. That was an invaluable benefit for a beginner in the luxury real estate market. I was able to work on building a solid reputation. That stat helped with those who hadn't known me previously, and helped with referrals.

2. **Find a way to vet out who may be a good referral and who may not be.**
    This is more cut-and-dry than you may think. Asking for referrals is
    something you should have no problem doing with a client, especially
    if you know you served them to the best of your ability and addressed
    all their needs. If the client says they will give you referrals, put them
    into your system to ask for them. If they never send you one, say over a
    six-month period, recognize that they are not a good use of your resources.
    Remain friendly, but move them to the occasional contact list. They are
    definitely not a hot referral lead source.

    Overall, when it comes to referrals, don't use up large amounts of time
    looking busy and acting like you're doing the right thing by repeatedly
    approaching the same people who've basically told you "no." Think
    strategically.

3. **Learn the art of networking.**
    To be an effective networker:

    1. **Realize it is a two-way street**
        Your networking is not all about "get, get, get." You also have
        to find a way to "give, give, give" referrals to your strongest,
        most reliable networking resources. I have no problems
        referring certain friends of mine for referrals in their areas
        of expertise, whether they are financial, fitness, or medical
        related.
    2. **Don't just toss a name someone else's way**
        It's not up to you to qualify a lead for someone else, but you
        should make sure you're not referring someone who is a time
        waster or not seriously interested in the service at some point,
        if not the present moment.
    3. **Go to events to talk to people you *don't* know**

I've been known to go to a networking event and end up talking with people I already know, not anyone new. Find ways to get in front of new people that are a good target audience for you. There'll be some intensive conversation about this in the chapter *Investing in You*.

4. **Strive toward creating an effective, powerful "contacts list"**
Is the network you market to filled with your high school buddies, your parents' pals, and random individuals who are not part of your target market? Don't kid yourself by thinking they are a part of meaningful career network. Keep them informed via occasional emails, etc., but don't count that email as something that is really working the system.

To build a business as a realtor, there is one thing you absolutely need—clients. Without them, none of it works. You have to take smart and strategic steps to build up your credibility, experience and goals while connecting with the right people. You might be the best realtor in the world—in your mind—but if no one ever learns that for themselves, it's nothing more than a pleasant fantasy.

FIGURE TO DO THESE 3 THINGS

There's no better way to cut through the haze and make sure you see a clear picture of what it takes to become the person you want to be in real estate, than blunt talk.

What I'd like you to enjoy is taking control of these three ideas to show you are not just another struggling realtor. You are serious and committed to the long haul, because honestly, both the industry and consumers need realtors.

1. **Don't strive for a home run on every deal.**

    Look at the big picture and think of the long haul. How many deals could you get if you took an approach that was reasonable with people? Because if you don't, someone else will. So, think about how many deals you can open up for your future by showing some compromise in the right situations, at the right time. A reduced commission for a good stat can be a great deal for your career trajectory. Take advantage of this!

2. **Be relational, not transactional.**

    If you think in terms of deals, and not in terms of building relationships, you are going to have to work harder and longer for every deal you get. You may be busy, and you may be "successful," but you're not going to start scoring the easy wins—which a well-cared for referral is.

    Make it a goal to build clients for life, and you'll develop relationships and friendships. This means reaching out monthly using your system. The old rule-of-thumb used to be to reach out every six months, but monthly is better. Visualize your past client at a cocktail party, talking about realtors and a home a friend wants to buy. Are they more likely to remember you five months later, or more easily if they just heard from you within the past few weeks?

3. **Be honest and insightful—the voice of professional reason.**

    When you are known as the compassionate and caring realtor who gives real information to your clients—both in exciting times and when a problem may arise—you'll be appreciated for it and stand out. Many times, people are emotionally charged-up during real estate transactions and when something goes wrong, they really want to know they are working with a proven realtor who will take on that burden for them and keep their cool at the same time. This is where you can honestly show your calm, collected head and be a solutions-oriented agent, not someone who causes tensions to rise even further. Half-in-the-game realtors simply cannot do this effectively. Your commitment to the long haul will pay off greatly in these types of situations.

The quality of a person's life is in direct proportion to their commitment to excellence, regardless of their chosen field of endeavor.

VINCE LOMBARDI

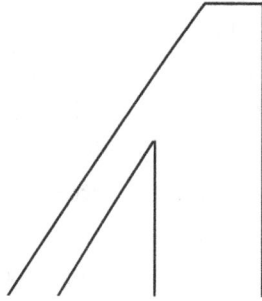

FIGURE TO SURROUND YOURSELF WITH GREATNESS

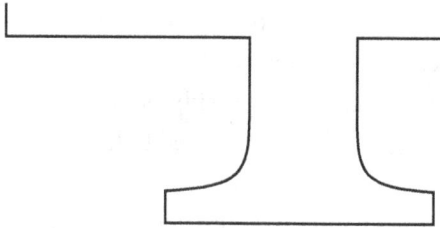

The people that want to step into
their greatness are hungry.

LES BROWN

Most of us are well versed about the suggested steps you can take to achieve greatness, and I am one of those people. I love to read and capture new ideas. However, I also believe the distinction between what has happened for me and what has yet to happen for others, is I actually strive to live the steps that lead to success. From the time with my mom's friends growing up onward, I have had the wonderful opportunity to be around some of the most inspiring people. They did great things, not just talk about great things, and that really had an impact on me.

I look back at high school and some of my social circles and see a group of people that really had no aspirations to do anything better with their life. They just weren't enthusiastic about their potential. For many of them, it ended up beating them down and I came close a time or two, but decided after a few close calls with bad decisions that I wanted to experience more. I grew serious about creating meaningful relationships with the right types of people—those people who were doing great things. I wanted to learn from them.

If you are the sum of your five best friends, you'd better make sure they add up to something.

As I began to learn and grow with a commitment focused on my personal growth and journey to my version of "greatness," I noticed a few significant things taking place around me:

1. Those who weren't driven for success in their own life began to slowly fade away.
2. I saw clearly how many people who have decided not to strive for more really do want you to settle for less—for whatever reason.

Because of these factors, our relationships drifted apart and while I had no ill will for these people, I had no desire to stay in the unchallenged world they were building for their lives.

Your greatness is linked to the greatness of those you surround yourself with. All the nuances of creating a life where you surround yourself with those who do great things in their lives, are going to be shared in this chapter.

YOUR CIRCLE OF CLOSEST FRIENDS

There is no greater friendship than
one that challenges you to grow
to your greatest potential.

***

CHRIS LACHARITY

Today, my circle of close friends are both enthusiastic and successful. I am not referring to financial success alone (although it comes with the initiative); I am talking about the energy of everyone I mostly associate with. I am confident in the referrals we share. The referral I offer will be received by someone that understands its value—a professional who doesn't just talk a good line, but is good through their actions too. That is the essence of greatness, in my opinion.

Are you wondering why your friends are so important to your career? If you are, contemplate this question:

Do you feel it is best to keep your personal circle of friends away from your professional circles of development? If your answer is yes, you may have tapped into one of the reasons why you are not gaining the success you'd like.

It's ineffective thinking to spend your energy trying to separate your personal circle from your professional success. More things could go wrong than right. For example:

1. If you run into a business prospect, how do you suddenly switch to the person you are when you're seeking out referrals and business in front of your friend?
2. If your friend(s) are doing something that wouldn't look good for you professionally and you are spotted by a client, how would that appear?

Once upon a time, it was a belief you should keep your personal and professional life separate. That wisdom came with good intentions, but if you are in sales and hoping to succeed, you should fully expect a referral or new opportunity could come your way at any minute. You don't want to waste opportunities for a potentially important introduction because you're not on your A-game because you're hanging around with your "no-game" friends.

Start to take notice if you have a group of friends who struggle to find what they are passionate about. Just because you were close friends once doesn't mean you owe them an obligation to hold back on your goals just because they may be struggling to identify any for themselves. Go out for a drink with them or meet up once in a while, but you should be mindful of your time, goals, and the energy you exude when doing that.

AUTHENTIC TRANSITIONS

You have committed to self-growth, both as a person and a professional, but you're starting out. The natural next thought is: *How am I going to make this happen*? I understand why you don't want to just cut out your friends that have been around a long time and turn your back on them. They were important to you at one time.

Your goal should be to develop greater relationships with the people who can positively affect you the most. Already successful individuals could potentially teach you valuable skills and information, and become valuable referral sources at some point. Since these are the people who've already done what you've set out to do, which is create new connections that help you fall into your own greatness, you'll want to show you are a person of value to them. The best ways I've seen this work include:

- **Be open-minded and energetic**
  It'll be discussed more in chapter 7 *Figure to Send the Elevator Back Down*, but successful people realize the importance of giving back to those who are on the rise. If you show you are seriously determined and have good energy and a desire to learn, that is often enough to earn an opportunity to engage with people who are "career and mind growers" in some capacity. You just have to make sure you don't pass these opportunities by. If you receive an invitation to a networking event and you had planned on going out for beers with the buddies—just like you do every Friday night—take a pass on the beers and go where your future could begin.

- **Focus on one person, not the entire group**
  It doesn't take diving into a group of people to get an opportunity to connect with greatness. If you have casually met or heard of one person that really interests you and you feel they have a good message to share, create a connection with that person first. Find out the best way to do that. Maybe it's a cup of coffee. Then be prepared to have a great conversation with them, which means you learn more about them first and ask questions. Then learn and absorb what they say! Your energy will show through and they will become a person who can comfortably promote you and help open some doors for you. Remember—people are glad to do these types of things for others they know are serious and committed.

- **Be authentic and educated**

  You can't go into an opportunity to surround yourself with greatness with a self-centered and self-absorbed attitude. You must be authentic and want to be there. Additionally, you'll want to show the proper respect for these peoples' time by being educated and well-versed in some important areas. For example, if you're in real estate, you are up-to-date with topics that are important to your market and industry. Show the people you want to associate with that you are vested in your career and are interested in what they have to say. This goes a long way and it's easy to do.

- **Don't dwell on age**

  I hang around with a fair number of people who are ten-to-fifteen years older than me, and they are some of my best friends. Others have commented on why I hang around with people so much older than me, and for me, it's easy. I hang around people that are energized and passionate about their lives. People who share meaningful stories and valuable teachings. Age is not a number that fits into my equation when it comes to great friendships because it's highly irrelevant. The same goes for a younger person that's energetic and passionate.

I want to touch upon the topic of age just a bit more. Mostly because I don't want you to discredit one of the greatest opportunities you may have to grow your success, which is the one that I believe comes through having friends who have already gone through the places you are headed.

One of the things I've discovered about my friendships with people older than myself is that they enjoy talking with me because they see their younger selves in me. I love to hear that and they share great information with me about their past struggles, which always creates good opportunities for perspective, at the least. For example, many times they'll tell me they really didn't make any money until they were in their mid-forties, maybe even older, and that makes me feel pretty great, because I'm not that age yet and I can see I'm on track.

As I gain expertise and grow, I am very excited to be the one who looks for the person younger than me who reminds me of where I once was.

Ultimately, your greatness is going to come from authenticity and internal self-work, combined with doing the things you love. This shows and it's contagious. I have a friend who thinks I'm the luckiest man in the world because I'm not married. He sees my success, takes note of my energy, and perceives me to have a really amazing lifestyle. I appreciate the way he talks about me and he actually introduces me to others in that same way, as well. However, I know it's not me being single that gives me this lifestyle. It's the people I associate with and the natural energy and drive they give me. When you're in sales, it's all about the people.

HOW TO MAKE ACQUAINTANCES FEEL LIKE FRIENDS

If you want others to like you, if you want to develop real friendships, if you want to help others at the same time as you help yourself, keep this principle in mind: Become genuinely interested in other people.

———————

DALE CARNEGIE

The entire process of real estate allows you to meet many people throughout your career—if you are experiencing success in it. You meet various people at showings, through your clients (insurance agents, other real estate agents, bankers, etc.) and at the closing. Each one of these times is a time to be aware of the power of connection you can create.

Even though you are meeting someone who may not be your client, you can leave a good impression that creates a connection with him or her. You are building an acquaintance, which could lead to creating a genuine friendship where the opportunity to conduct more business with that person could eventually exist.

There are a few realtors in my market that I've met a time or two, mostly at showings. I'm a curious guy and I have asked them questions, started conversations, and did my part to make it an energetic and engaged showing. I consider it a networking event, of sorts, and although everyone knows what I do by that point, it's a chance to relationship-build for the future. Remember, you just never know when a good opportunity could come your way. And, just because someone used a realtor one time does not mean they will remember them the next time they need one (particularly if they don't follow a system). So, for me, this approach has paid off because of the impression it leaves.

Aside from the potential for future clients, it has also led many of the realtors to believe we are good friends. This isn't always true, but it perfectly demonstrates the importance of how you impress yourself upon others. Through your sincerity, energy, and passion for what you do, you can leave a positive and lasting impression in every situation.

A side benefit of this:

When you represent yourself sincerely and with energy for what you do, it often comes back as a pick-me-up when you may need it most. I'm vulnerable, just like we all are, to those days where my flow is off. And it takes just a simple compliment such as "Chris, he's the best," to remind me of how fortunate I am. The best part is that these things come my way naturally—always at the right time.

YOUR SELF-PERCEIVED GREATNESS

I am someone who has fallen victim to my own negative thoughts and words. Poor self-talk is a huge challenge for anyone who is aspiring for greatness because everything about it works against what you are hoping to achieve.

It has been difficult to start lessening this type of inner chatter, and while I cannot say I know where it came from, exactly, I do recognize I am very hard on myself. If things don't go perfectly in a transaction, I am my toughest critic. If anyone else were to say anything, there is a good chance I have already thought it—and worse. But I also recognize this is an obstacle worth getting over, because it will hold me back.

They say that what you think you are, you become, and I know I'm working on big goals that have no room for those statements that involve negative words and ideas.

There are days when I do not want to dive right into my work when my day begins. My sister works for me now and she'll come in so happy and ask how I am. Honestly, it's hard for me to not feel like a curmudgeon. I just want to do what I have to do, and not participate in that type of talk. However, I do realize those moments are an opportunity for me to show my greatness and not allow any negative thought deter me or influence my day. It will take a lot longer to undo any negative action I may cultivate than it takes to collect myself and engage positively. Today, I just remind myself to be positive and I can switch gears to that preferred state, and I'm mostly successful at it.

5 STEPS TO BUILD GREATNESS

When you take steps that constantly move you forward, they become more manageable and increase your chances of success. Taking the steps to build greatness in your life is a challenge you should embrace. Remember...there are five steps to help you keep it real and practice greatness in your career and life.

1. **Be honest with yourself.**
   I think mostly everyone has lied to themselves about their efforts for success, including myself. We all say and think we work hard and do all these things toward our success, so when it doesn't happen fast enough, we wonder why it isn't working.

   This is when you need to get honest and break it down. The real picture often reveals we could be doing ten-times more than what we are currently doing, or at least, work smarter. How do you really spend your days? This is what you have to figure out. Start by asking yourself a few questions:

   1. In the past months, how many times have I skipped out on a networking opportunity because I just "didn't feel like it" that day?
   2. How many distractions do I allow into my day? For example: do I check every text or email immediately or do I finish what I'm involved in before doing that?
   3. How well do I follow my system every day?
   4. What are the number of hours I actually spend on my career, and not other matters?
   5. How much of my personal life do I carry with me to the office?
   6. When I am talking with others, am I talking in a pro-growth way or is it a complaining session?

Honesty can be brutal, but it is the best way to understand what your real efforts have been. And once you know your role, you can start to make shifts if you're really serious about developing your personal greatness.

2. **Evaluate the people you talk to the most in a day.**

Be conscious of who you call or give your time to I always had a great relationship with my broker owners since they were typically positive, high energy people who wanted the best for me. I always admired the tremendous energy of those people. Marilyn Wilson and Donald Abraham are two people that always gave me their time and support which I will always remember and appreciate. As busy as life gets I try to recharge with like-minded friends that are striving for excellence. Again be conscious of who wants the best for you and keep those who do very close to you. I mention my relationship with Tony Greco throughout this book. Even though we are in different businesses they have a connection and similarities. Both real estate and the fitness industry are tough to succeed in but the sky is the limit if you have the vision and work ethic to create something huge! Speak to people daily who share your passion for success. Appreciate all you have achieved but support each other to take it as far as you can. You'll be surprised how much your support will boost the confidence of even your most successful friends. We all need the reassurance of the ones that know us best.

Whom do you talk to most in a day? When you are working and trying to garner your greatness for success, you cannot spend your productive time surrounded by personal dramas and situations that distract you from reaching your fullest potential. Discipline is required in this area and it is not easy—but it is necessary! Occasionally there may be an exception to the rule, but that should be rare. If you are stressed out about either your own or someone else's personal issues every day, or in a constant state of stress and crisis, you cannot give your best to your career. Your growth will be stifled and you will have more personal struggles than you would otherwise. This is why you have to come up with a system that allows you to manage these situations during times when it won't affect your work.

3. **Eliminate your fears that hold you back.**
   Many times, we stifle our growth because we may fear some part of it. However, it is only through continuing to learn and challenge ourselves that we can build more confidence, become a more knowledgeable individual, and really become that person of greatness other people take notice of.

   One of the biggest fears people have is that of public speaking. In fact, some people are less afraid of dying than public speaking—it's that bad. Regardless of your career or if you ever plan to deliver a big speech to an audience, overcoming your fear of public speaking is a benefit for you. Conquering this barricade of a fear would be time well spent, because if you can speak to a large group without worry, you can more easily speak to people one-on-one with more confidence too.

   When fear holds you back, it is difficult to experience the success and fulfillment you seek. If you don't deal with it, you will continue to carry it around with you. It can sap your energy and leave you with less drive. By overcoming fear, you give yourself the opportunity to recognize your fullest potential—that nothing has to hold you back if you don't want it to.

4. **Continuously learn and improve.**
   You need to learn to improve. Doing anything besides this is putting a limit on your potential and possibilities. You open up opportunities when you know a great deal that is going on within your field of sales. For me, when I walk into a room to meet with people for a listing, in particular, I know I will receive many questions people want answered, and whether or not they pertain to my role as a realtor is irrelevant. If I don't know the answers, I have failed. When I know the answers, I welcome the questions, build the rapport, and show that I am a committed professional.

People are going to test you and you should expect this—and welcome it. You won't know everything in a day, but once you start passing all those tests, you'll love being the "go-to" source for questions. I surrounded myself with knowledgeable realtors once I seriously committed to my career, and with that came the expectation I would be disciplined enough to make sure I was the person who did have answers.

As you grow into your fullest potential as a realtor, you should accept the fact there will always be competitors, changing markets, and people who test you. These things are incredible motivators when you take serious and massive action to grow your career.

EFFECTIVE NETWORKING

Referrals aren't given easily. If you don't take the time to establish credibility, you're not going to get the referral. People have to get to know you. They have to feel comfortable with who you are and what you do.

IVAN MISNER

The main purpose of networking is to grow your base of potential contacts. In turn, if you do this right and build rapport with people, it should also increase your rate of referrals. Networking is all about the art of creating a connection with people, and it can be challenging to do.

At times, you could start talking with a person, only to quickly discover they are a time-waster who just wants to talk.

At other times, a person may approach you that catches you off guard. You won't be invested in the conversation, although they are.

Also, you can meet fantastic and interesting people when you are networking and have them like you right away, and you like them too. But it's just friendly and there really isn't any opportunity for business growth.

However…what keeps sales people going are those times when the conversation aligns and you realize you have this energy upon which to build a good relationship. And by building that relationship, you guessed it…the referrals will begin to flow both ways. You can't go into the whole deal with a 'refer me to everyone' attitude and not know how to feel out a decent referral to send their way at some point.

Networking isn't always my favorite thing, because I am committed to maximizing my time. In reality, networking has become an important part of my time to grow my business.

The way I have found success is not by going to networking parties, or those events where you spend five minutes with each business person getting to know each other. Swapping cards is not networking, and from what I've experienced, these are people who are learning to network and have nothing to offer you. If you need to practice your networking skills, great; otherwise, just avoid these and go to where the difference-makers are—the people who have reached the point of greatness.

For example, if I were an agent who was selling semi-detached homes in the suburbs, I'd go to kids' fairs and all those types of events to network. But that isn't my market. For my market, I need to talk with people who are in a different league of success. For me, the opportunities I need to seek out are with the "who's who" of the community. I don't always want to go, but I know I have to go to those places where I'll find these individuals. So, I put on a suit and get ready to go in, placing myself in the mindset of knowing I'll have a good time once I get there. That part is easy to do, because I always do enjoy myself once I'm engaged in the process.

Getting to the networking event is one thing, creating a "pro-business growth" conversation is quite another.

I am guilty of getting caught-up in long conversations in the corner of the room at networking events—with people whom I already know. This completely defeats the purpose, of course, and if you don't get out there and talk to other people, you are really just wasting your time, which means you need to revisit how honest you are being with yourself. If you get a new lead and your gut tells you there is potential there, great! One strong lead is significant towards success. However, if you are talking to the same old people who are at every event—only talking to each other and never anyone else—you need to do whatever it takes to grow out of that. Don't risk growing stagnant.

As I mentioned, this is a struggle with me at times because I am busy. There are groups of people I see at these events that I enjoy catching up with. However, I know this—I'd never go hang out with them socially even though I like them. That reveals something important to me: they are not the ones who I am meant to invest so much time into, not when I should be networking.

The Best Strategy

Walk in alone to a networking event so you don't have a good friend or colleague there as a crutch. Smile, make eye contact, and remember you don't go up to someone to talk about you, you do so to find out about them.

And be aware of this…

When you go to real estate school they will have sections regarding networking that are quite antiquated. They no longer apply, and if those techniques really worked, the teacher would still be an active and successful real estate agent. It is fine to choose teaching, of course, because some people are passionate about that aspect of real estate. We need them! However, if you want to master networking you go to the person who has mastered networking for wisdom. It's more complicated than saying, "Just do this…and you'll get this…"

ASKING FOR REFERRALS

One customer, well taken care of, could be more valuable than $10,000 worth of advertising.

JIM ROHN

Being in sales means you must also be comfortable to ask for referrals. Why wouldn't you? Especially if you:

1. Take care of your clients;
2. Are ethical and committed to giving best efforts;
3. And, experience satisfied clients that are grateful to you.

The point is, if you have created a good connection, you need to ride that wave and see if people are going to refer others to you. If they say "no," then you have something solid to go off than if you never even ask. A "no" means one of two things:

1. There is a reason they are hesitant to refer you;
2. They don't like to refer people;

With the first option, try to find out why they might be hesitant. It will provide you with a good opportunity to learn something that may help your career in the future. With the "I don't refer people" type of answer, you should probably believe them. You can't talk someone into giving quality referrals. The best you can do is say, "I understand, but if that ever changes and someone needs a realtor, please contact me." Then they go on your newsletter list and occasional follow-ups, end of story (unless something changes).

You'll also find some people who like to place their requests for referrals as tag lines on their business cards. It doesn't hurt, but how can you know your card will be right there in that person's possession when they have an opportunity to refer someone? You can't hope for that or rely on it for a business strategy. Plus, a tagline—whether clever or not—is not enough for many people to act and refer you. One of my most favorite innovators in real estate training is Brian Buffini, and he's absolutely successful. His tagline is "I'm never too busy for your referrals." For me, that line doesn't work, but I would never argue against his success with it. The reason I bring this up is I have seen how relying on a tagline to get business seldom works, and it can leave an unfavorable impression of you on others. What you thought was clever, may be thought of as unprofessional or an uninspiring message.

One time when I was getting my haircut I was talking about what motivates me to my barber, and as we got going with it, I brought up an analogy that I use quite often.

Imagine this…

You have a spouse or friend that is kidnapped and you have 365 days to get $1M ransom to get them back. You don't have a million dollars! What would you do? Would you go out and ask every one of your friends to help you out? You sure would.

But then your logical mind steps in and you're thinking, *but I'm not going to go out and ask everyone for money because I don't have a loved one who has been kidnapped.* My response to that is, "If you are in real estate you should ask all your friends and clients for referrals." They may still resist, but it all comes down to asking this question:

If you or anyone else you know ever looks to buy or sell a home, would I be the realtor of choice that you'd recommend they use?

If you don't hear a resounding "yes," don't take it personally. Just remove this person from your database and begin to seek out those who will give you referrals. Because once you get a referral and take great care of that individual, a flood of referrals is more likely to come your way. Your actions as a realtor make the one who referred your client look good. We all like to look good, right? You really need to use some common sense when asking.

1. Don't butt in and ask for a referral and interrupt another conversation;
2. Gauge the person's mood, as someone in a bad or distracted mood is not someone you want to ask about referrals at that moment;
3. Be polished and professional when you ask so you know there is no doubt in their minds you are serious;
4. And, don't change your disposition if your request doesn't go the way you'd hoped. Remain professional or you'll lose any chance of opening that doorway in the future at a better time.

Once referrals begin to work for you, people will actually come and ask you what type of clients you take. Recently, I had a gentleman ask me what my referral criteria was, assuming I didn't touch anything under a million dollars. I said, "Absolutely not. You have to specialize in something and I happen to specialize in million-dollar-plus properties, but I do everything, including rentals." When someone has an inaccurate perception of your business scope it is important for them to know you appreciate this other type of business just as much as the million-dollar-home buyer or seller.

My appreciation for the value of referrals is of such a great magnitude that I have committed to never letting someone down—never, regardless of what it takes. This may seem like a foolhardy pursuit, but I have a very good reason for it. It goes back to what I touched upon earlier, the wisdom about making sure that when someone is referred to me, the one giving the referral will not end up with a negative feed back about my services.

I don't expect anyone to refer me just because I am a real estate agent, nor am I going to pay someone cash under the table—not just because it's illegal, but because it demeans my value. I want to be referred because others know I'm the best. So, I go out of my way to ensure people are happy and have no doubts I am the best.

The reason I do this is the harsh reality of how referrals work. I could pull off fifteen miracles, but people will remember the one that went awry. That is human nature. However, to me, a referral is the greatest compliment and to goof it up is unacceptable. It all comes down to the referral source and their value, and at times that means more than the money. This is true whether it's a first referral or someone who refers regularly. Every referral is golden.

Does this cause stress at times? Absolutely, and that's when I have to remember to take care of myself. Things *can* get overwhelming. I am not obsessive-compulsive in all things, but when it comes to business, I need structure and discipline. As I write this, just last night I'd forgotten I offered a ticket to a hockey game for two different people. One was let down because they'd been excited to go. It killed me. Yet other things, such as unreasonable expectations, don't bother me as much as forgetting about that extra hockey ticket.

At times, you also have to be honest with your referral source. You can't share personal information with them about the transaction, but you can give an overview if there are some hurdles. That is okay to do and your engagement with the process can help you keep the referral source happy, and that relationship intact.

Other referral sources are meant to go by the wayside, as well. My sister used to refer me people all the time and they were often very challenging people.

After a while, it looked like it was me. It wasn't. There is an art to giving a proper referral and you never want to be known as "the guy who can do anything."

It's also important to remember referrals are supposed to be reciprocated. If you took advantage of a referral that dropped the ball on you, would you refer people to that source? Not if you really valued your referrals, you wouldn't. The entire process should make people look good and give a client a specific product or service they need, and have them leave the experience grateful for it. And if things go wrong, hopefully the opportunity for constructive criticism exists, because that is what will help to fix the problem or else recognize that the referral relationship is not there, at least from your end. I do have people I no longer refer to that still refer to me, so it can go one way, even though two ways is ideal.

FIGURE TO DO THESE 3 THINGS

All you need to remember is that greatness begins with you.

1. **Take an inventory of your life.**
    Determine if you are committed to what you want to do. When that agent asked me if I was 100% committed, he was spot on. I hadn't been fully in the game, although I said I was. At first, I resisted but over time, I saw why he asked the question. As you reflect on your life, have you had anyone ask you similar questions? If you did, how did you respond? It may be time to revisit those questions and you'll find a different answer.

2. **Maximize your time.**
    Most of us have busy schedules, and realtors definitely do. You spend a lot of time driving around in your car and find gaps of time between meetings that shouldn't be spent doing nothing. For me, if I have to drive to the west end of town for appointments, I always make sure I have

errands in that area I can do at the same time. Simple strategies like this save me many valuable hours a week.

3. **Determine whom you are drawn to and what their influence is on you, and vice versa.**

   It really is important to evaluate your social circles, as they are intricately linked to a real estate career. It takes more than a genuine desire and putting in a full week's worth of work to grow your real estate career. So, when you have those valuable opportunities to be in a room filled with potential referrals, make sure the time counts. Are you only listening to everyone, or do you have something to say? It should be a combination of both, and what you hear should help you grow; what you share should help others grow. This is a necessary component of greatness.

> When you are ready to make a shift in your career trajectory, the day to start is today. Not next week, the first of the month, or some other time—today!

CHRIS LACHARITY

5

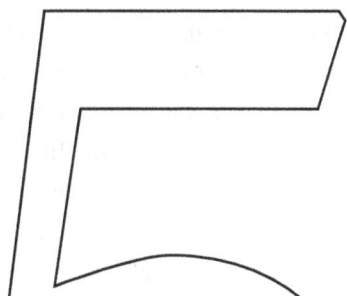

FIGURE TO CUTTING THE BS

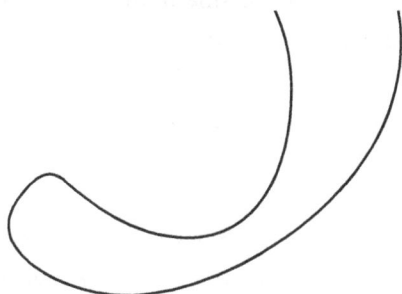

If it is important to you, you will find
a way. If not, you'll find an excuse.

DANIEL DECKER

W're surrounded by so many excuses about *why* it's not the right time, or poor them, or they're not that type of person. Most of us have said or thought something similar, just as most of us have heard someone else say the same thing. There are no positive responses to those negative thoughts and words, which really are excuses.

When you eliminate excuses, you naturally increase your focus and discipline. I know most of us try to do the right things and follow the wisdom we read in books like this. Maybe you're doing six of the seven figures after you read this and act, but things still are not fully connecting. When you think about what's missing, it's likely the one figure you decided not to become disciplined in (for whatever the reason).

Your work ethic is in direct correlation to the amount of BS you have going on.

It would be ideal if you could just have all the successes without the work, but that will never happen. Your hard work has to have value and when you make excuses, you are lowering your value. With my big goals, I am constantly evaluating if I really am doing everything I need to do to reach them, or if I'm kidding myself in certain areas. This can take a lot of conscious effort to do at first, because it presents the risk of you exposing where you've fallen short.

You have to schedule your days to maximize them, and if you do this and hold yourself accountable for your every step, you'll find:

1. You follow your system and make your calls;
2. Your clients know they are being tended to professionally;
3. You grow new leads and referrals;
4. You get time to do the things important to you;
5. And, you can still have time for some fun if you so choose to.

You want to make your time count. Are you wasting time or doing whatever you can to arrive at your goals, whatever they may be? I'm a huge advocate of overshooting my goals, which means that when I'm going for a million-dollar year, I'm going to think about a two-million-dollar year. Then, in the end, the target goal will be reached.

Are you wondering, why not just go for the target goal? You know what it is anyway. There is a good reason for going beyond it. When you get a system in place and everything starts moving and you're fully committed (no excuse mode), suddenly big things can begin to happen quickly. You may exceed your goal, which is an awesome reward to experience.

THERE WILL ALWAYS BE POTENTIAL DISTRACTIONS

When you are focused on a task, you have to be able to shut out the distractions hurled at you. They are nonstop, which is why if you focus on success, you must be prepared for everything.

CHRIS LACHARITY

There you are sitting at your desk, trying to put together a market analysis for a property you're going to present on that night. Your phone rings and you automatically pick it up, mid-thought, and answer. It's a question about another property listing you have, and you answer the question and try to get more insights, only to find out the person works with another realtor already. Okay, you hang up and get back to your project. A few minutes later, a text shows up on your cell phone. Your friend wants to know if you can go golfing later that week. You text back that week won't work and then you banter back and forth before ending the stream.

Now you look down at your market analysis again and see that about one new line has been added and you've lost fifteen minutes. You have to leave for an appointment in an hour, and you're not sure how you'll get back to finish the document and print it off before going to your appointment that night. Maybe you can reschedule something…

Does this self-induced distraction sound familiar? It happens to everyone in all professions, but for a realtor, whose livelihood depends on their knowledge and the level of service they offer their clients and potential clients, distractions can stop your momentum dead in its tracks.

You need a system you can follow that helps you to avoid distractions in the present and begins to work for you to repeat your successes in the future.

TRAINING YOUR MIND FOR SUCCESS

The key to success is to focus our conscious mind on things we desire not things we fear.

BRIAN TRACY

No matter what you have in mind for your goal, whether it's immense like my goals in business are (by my standards), or big to you, you still must have a strategy that resonates with you. Your mind must accept it and that has a purpose; to help you develop the resilience to ensure you work toward your results every day. It should get to the point where it's not a question of *if* you'll do it, but *when* you'll do it. The best way to do this is to map out your day so you see it right there in front of you and your brain evaluates it and knows what it is supposed to be doing for that day. This way you can also overcome anxiety better.

This past year I had my best January ever, and I was so excited. Despite that, the accomplishments of that month still left me feeling anxious about what would happen in February. How could I make that continue? This is how I think. Others think this way too and still others may think more vaguely, such as:

1. Who cares what happens in February! After all, January was a killer month.
2. It's impossible to be that busy in February if you were that busy in January. There is only so much time in a day.
3. You were still successful. That should be reward enough.

All of these sentiments could be true. However, they are not ones that show a commitment to a goal or that you have the mindset that you will do what it takes to work towards your goal. That's why mapping out your day is so important. The way I do this is by:

- **Thinking of every month as a personal goal I need to reach my desired achievement.**
  This means I have to create a new list every month with important details surrounding these questions:

  1. Whom can I contact on my list?
  2. How many people can I close?
  3. What will it take to make the money I require to reach my goal?

I'll stress again it's not all about the money, per se, but when you are in real estate your success is gauged by the commissions you earn, as well as the other things you can show (statistics, target market expertise, etc.). And again, focusing on your financial gain is not bad. After all, if you are successful you can do many things to help other people with your money—things that are good for individuals and the world, at large. It's a way of paying it forward that's based on your success.

- **Finding a referral "wing man."**
  My friend Tony Greco is outstanding at introducing people he trusts with business and referrals more masterfully than anyone else I've ever come across. He can speak so highly of you to someone else right in front of you and make it sound perfectly natural. If you can find a source for referrals like this—a great friend who generates great leads due to their energy—take advantage of a wonderful lifelong friend. And reciprocate, of course. What's great about this, aside from a great friendship and referrals, is that nothing says you are serious (and not a realtor full of BS) more than getting a referral and introduction from someone whose opinion matters greatly to people of affluence.

- **Never abandon your system and plan.**
  It would be easy to fool yourself into thinking that having lunches and breakfasts for leads could take you to your goal every month, but you'd be misled to believe that. It is not always the most effective use of your productive time. A breakfast with one person is not an equal substitute to following up with 25 emails, notes, or phone calls a day. You have to do both.

When it comes to excuse-making, abandoning the system becomes one of the first casualties of it. If your networking breakfast runs over, you suddenly decide to not make any calls that day or use up all your time to send your emails that morning—but never play catch-up. This is a costly mistake, as the odds of new referrals will decrease, just by the law of numbers, when you abandon your system. Additionally, you need to be honest with yourself and realize that calls, notes, and emails are by far the easiest part of your day. If you can't do the easier "stuff," how will you ever master the tougher challenges?

Please, just do not kid yourself that "fake work" is real work. You have to be selective and deliberate in what you do. This also includes absorbing yourself too much into properties that are not in your area of expertise. One thing I do is refer some of the clients I have for lower-end homes, or that have more demanding needs (than what works for me), to agents that work for me. They are grateful for the opportunity and take excellent care of the clients. Ultimately, it is important, as well as good practice, to step aside when you can't serve a client properly. Don't be stubborn—just bring in another individual you have confidence in to take care of them. That's what you do when you really care about the client's experience.

I want to share the personal criteria I use to determine if I should have a breakfast or lunch meeting suggested to me. This is the best way I have found to determine if I can both bring and receive value to the hour to hour-and-a-half I book out.

The guidelines for this style of networking are:

1. I try to make sure there are at least three people in the meeting. This way, if I am not connecting with one person, I can perhaps connect with the other. You can do this in a very easy-going manner that isn't obvious or distasteful. Opportunity happens all the time when you put yourself in the right spot. Which, let's be frank, is the place where the deal makers go to have lunch.
2. I will have at least two items on my agenda that I'd like to discuss. This is where I can create distinction by bringing value to the table. You also avoid looking like a time-waster

because you offer more than fluff (a.k.a false statements); you are offering information you feel could genuinely benefit your audience.

The other day I was having lunch with a great friend and there were four contractors in the corner also having lunch. They were talking about how one of my competitors had let them down—of course, I had not known that. The owner of the restaurant heard them and knew who I was and came over and told me. Then he made an introduction that led to one of the gentlemen coming to sit at my table for a bit, and eventually I made my way over to their table. Unexpectedly, I was with four potential connections and I had something of value to share with them to fill a void they had. This is ideal, and it doesn't have to be the exception to the rule if you follow the system.

In that group were four valuable potential referral sources—a builder, an architect, a client, and a banker. I knew if I could resonate with one of them, it would be a successful venture and I'd have found a person that would take my call. So, I answered questions liberally and asked about their situations, perspectives, and dilemmas, knowing that if I resonated with one of these people, it was time wisely invested. I shared how I could make a difference and talked about the stats, speaking from my heart in an unrehearsed way. The more you feel and experience success, the simpler it becomes to do this because it's authentic—a part of you that you can share without any BS. In the end, a nice lunch with a great friend ended up turning into a meeting that was an excellent use of my time.

Another hint that can let you know if people are sincere in their interest or wasting your time is if they value their time. Someone who has nowhere to go is likely someone who is going nowhere in the referral department.

Make sure you are also aware of how valuable your time is. For example, if you factor in a ten-hour work day and have a goal of a million in commissions for the year, that means you are at an hourly value rate of about $360 dollars.

To ensure you're on track, simply ask yourself: is this time going to lead to generating that type of rate? If the answer is "no," you know and you can move on. If the answer is "yes," you can put the contact into your system and take advantage of what may come next from your mutual energy and interest in doing business together.

Sometimes you need to look beyond what a lunch can do for you in the moment. Another lunch client had already decided to work with another realtor, but I still wanted to have lunch with him as I had some ideas to discuss that went beyond his deal (although I'll never give up hoping that I am that next realtor he needs). He was surprised I was willing to buy him lunch, but it ended up being very successful and productive for everyone. I made a valuable introduction to him for someone who could help him, while also keeping the referral network open for me. It's important to remember you should *never assume* just because someone works with another realtor they will not give you referrals. Being someone's realtor is no guarantee you're the only person on their mind when it comes to real estate. Again, you're not filling your mind with nonsense; you are doing something valuable with your time. In the end, that hour spent was a great deal for me, it generated exciting new income goals.

Every realtor has a different market to master with different nuances. You have to know the best way to maximize that through a combination of experimentation, research, and looking at what the successful realtors in your market do. Where do they go? This is a question not a hint.

DON'T KID YOURSELF—MONEY MATTERS

*Making money is art and working is art
and good business is the best art.*

—————————

ANDY WARHOL

I've mentioned this several times already, but it is truly important for you to understand. You don't have to feel guilty about wanting to make a lot of money if that is your goal. You can still make a lot of money and be genuine, kind, and a great asset to your world and to the lives of those you meet every day.

Is life all about money? Absolutely not. I am not all about money, but I know that it can bring me tremendous freedom. If you say life isn't about money and use that as a reason why you are not making a lot of money, you're creating an excuse as to why you are not successful. If you are saying you're as successful as you'd like to be that is fantastic, but chances are, if you're reading this book you're looking for a little bit more. So, be honest with yourself and embrace the good qualities of money. You don't have to sell a part of your soul in exchange for money; you can be a great person and also have wealth.

With money, you can have experiences that help you grow and work toward financial freedom. These are things most people want. No one thinks, *I am so excited to work until I die because I need the money.* Most people would like to earn their successes as early as possible so they can do two things:

1. Experience financial freedom;
2. And, have opportunities to do more while they are younger, rather than waiting.

The bonus is that when you are honest with yourself and have discipline to earn success, you will find it is an easier process to repeat. As has been expressed: <u>it's always hardest to make your first million</u>. From there, you have a formula and if you are prudent, you don't have to worry about those details of living day-to-day while you make your goals become your recognized successes.

THAT FIRST TASTE OF YOUR EFFORTS

My single greatest month of success in real estate has happened as I write this book, and because of that, I got some free media attention. It was an honor and humbling for me, but also a good bit of publicity to receive. Now my name is associated with big goals and since it was a highly successful project, it's an opportunity-in-the-making to expand on the potential that situation created. After all, I do have a lot more months coming up where making that same goal is practically mandatory.

For some people, one great month means they shut down a bit and stop riding the wave. As you have learned, that is the absolute wrong time to do that. You have to capitalize on these good fortunes and keep moving forward. You can't control everything, but when you're loyal to your system you can have it working for you when you're busy closing other deals. That's one of the most brilliant things about a good system.

Back when I was selling cars, I remember the song-and-dance routine so familiar to people in that industry. It happened toward the end of each month when it came down to "crunch time." I'd always begin to make my calls then. I'd make a list of my top ten clients I could possibly close and then go through that list. I'd go through it and shorten it after doing some research to see if they were really a party that could close a car deal by the end of the month. I'd usually end up with about six names on the list after that, and out of that, I would get three more deals at the end of the month. That method worked for me personally, and it has worked in real estate too.

My office is a visually stimulated graphic of my goals. I have chalkboard-painted walls and white boards everywhere. Each one of these boards has something of value that is right in front of my face, and when I'm on the phone

I can look up and reference specific properties to specific buyers. All sorts of information is at hand. For you, knowing this shows you a few valuable points that are exceptional to have in the real estate business:

1. I was really listening when they spoke;
2. I am organized and write down what potential clients share with me;
3. And, their business is of value to me.

I use these boards to help me work my next month's sales. I will hone in with a laser-like focus and make that list. If someone is lukewarm, I move on to the next. I keep going with my top prospects until either they tell me a firm no or they decide to buy/sell. And, if there is a client that is hot and then cold, flaking out and becoming high maintenance, I set them aside for the time being, or eliminate them all together if I intuitively feel they will never make a decision. It may seem crazy to remove people from your database, but you are better off having twenty truly interested parties than a hundred who will never do anything, no matter what.

DON'T ASSUME YOU'RE NOT GETTING BSed

Always remember that buyers/sellers don't always have the same habits as you. They may have no problem having you drive them around for a day to look at homes and not be the least bit serious. Do whatever you can to avoid falling into these time traps! Sadly, clients can be full of BS, as well, and it's okay to cut that part of it out of your day too!

CHRIS LACHARITY

Most clients are truly well-intended individuals who are interested in buying or selling their home if they contact you. It's great to know information and to understand the process; however, it is required a certain level of due diligence as a realtor to ensure you are not just appeasing their desire for attention and you are actually working toward a legitimate deal.

Situations are not always going to be what they first appear to be. Understanding this is a part of not counting a deal as closed until it actually is. This means:

1. **Don't confuse a credit pre-approval with an official bank approval.** Full approvals are dependent upon verification, appraisals, and a slew of other factors. A pre-approval mostly assumes accurate information was relayed, based on a credit report. Problems happen across the board—even in my target price range.

2. **Make sure the people you take to look at properties do not have a representation agreement with another realtor.**

   If you do this, it's ethically wrong and also a waste of your time. If those clients decided to purchase that home, guess who is getting paid? It's not you, it's the one with the agreement. Although many agents are a bit lax with having these agreements, there is value in them because it shows a buyer's firm commitment to you, which is positive. I assure you, they will most likely be looking at homes when you're not around (via the internet, open houses, driving by a home, etc.).

3. **Don't always show you'll be instantly available for clients.**

   At times, there will be clients or random individuals that will call you up if you have a listing and say something like, "I'm outside this house and want to look at it. Can you meet me here right now?" If you have nothing going on, you may consider it, but be cautioned, it could set up a precedent that you can't keep up with. Additionally, if you ask them if they're working with a realtor, they may say "yes," but the agent couldn't get there. You may want the sale, but it may not be wise to do. But if you want to, revert back to the previous bullet point. I know I very seldom readjust my schedule or drop what I'm doing to meet with someone who makes this type of demand. It will not only throw my schedule off but set up the illusion that I have nothing going on with my time—which is absolutely not accurate.

   Creating good, repeatable relationships is what you are looking to achieve in every deal you do. Sure, some people may only be one-time clients, and they are certainly still valuable, but you want to make sure you're not being intentionally misled by a client and showing how hungry you are for the commission that you don't care. I've found the best way to avoid this scenario circles back to receiving a majority of your clients via referral—good referrals have already vetted you out to the potential client and are more likely to not be working with anyone else.

THE POWER OF GRATITUDE

Gratitude can transform common days into thanksgivings, turn routine jobs into joy, and change ordinary opportunities into blessings.

WILLIAM A. WARD

I realize the importance of gratitude, and recognize I fail at showing the proper amount at times, because I am so tough on myself. Admitting the work you need in any area can be tough to do, but I am grateful I can admit my weaknesses and I am also smart enough to work on neutralizing them, if not turn them into a personal strength.

As a realtor, here are a few things I find gratitude in that you may also see as beneficial in helping you manage stress, work toward your future goals, and appreciate the opportunities before you every single day.

1. **Be thankful for those slower moments.**
    I have a list of things I can do when it is slower that help me grow personally and help with my business, as well. This list changes, but some of these examples are: reorganizing personal filing systems, taking a continuing education class, or evaluating your system and making updates to it you believe would be beneficial.

2. **Appreciate your opportunity to earn success every day.**
    If you are open to it happening, a good opportunity can happen for you every day. Or at least the seeds to put it into motion, can be planted. Many times, these seeds sprout when you least expect it.

3. **Realize you are always doing good things for you to grow.**
   Take care of yourself with diet and exercise. It's not always easy to eat healthy when you are out at lunches, working odd hours, and doing things where you don't have time to properly prepare a meal. However, you still have the ability to make sure you have good food to take with you on the go to give you more energy for your day.

4. **Celebrate the easy victories.**
   Whether it's not hitting red lights all the way across town or getting that easy "fall into your lap" deal, be grateful that you received that gift. All these great little things add up to a lot.

For some reason, I find it harder to be grateful for the big things, such as material possessions or monetary goals. Small things like walking my dog in the morning (shout out to Enzo, my Pug), is what I appreciate. Enzo makes me happy and provides me laughs daily. I am grateful for my comfortable existence and an opportunity to pause and lift my face up to the sun. Everyday experiences are the best source of gratitude and joy.

FIGURE TO DO THESE 3 THINGS

Key to your success will be to hold yourself accountable for everything you do. In fact, with writing this book I am holding myself accountable to my goal. I find this to be powerful because I assure you, it motivates me even when I am feeling a bit tired to keep moving forward. It inspires me to help myself, which in turn, can help you. This message is at the heart of the three things I want you to figure out doing.

1. **Write down your goal.**

   You're fooling yourself if you don't know where you're going or how you'll get there. By writing down your goals, you are beginning the process and making a start that will guide you to achieving it.

   Note: Do not make it complicated because that will most likely make it feel unmanageable.

2. **Put a timeline on your goal.**

   If you have a goal to do something big and don't put a timeline on it, you really don't have a goal, as much as a thought of something you'd like. Goals need to have end dates—even long-term goals.

   Note: Your timeline should be reasonable, dependent on the goal and your skill set at its start.

3. **Understand how you will implement your goal.**

   For me, stating my goals to my friends and people I meet is the single greatest way I ensure I'm doing something to implement my goal. When friends ask me, "Well, what happens if you don't reach it?" I reply, "That's not an option." They like the answer. And there have been some people who have been flippant about my goals in real estate and with this book, but I don't let that dissuade me or second guess myself. In fact, I use it to propel me forward. That's what you have to do, as well.

   Note: Don't let anyone's words take your energy or desire to achieve your goals. They are yours for the taking and making—no one else's.

You are your own best BS meter—both in your life and in the people you allow around you. If you remember that as you go through your journey, you'll be a step ahead of many people. Remember—no excuses, no retreat, no failure.

Ambition is the path to success. Persistence
is the vehicle in which you arrive.

_____

BILL BRADLEY

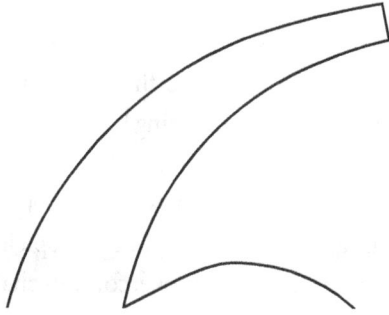

FIGURE TO OVERCOME OBSTACLES

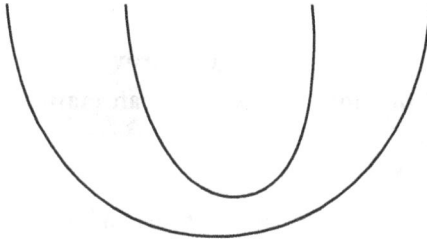

If you can find a path with no obstacles,
it probably doesn't lead anywhere.

FRANK A. CLARK

There are going to be obstacles every day. Take reading this book for example; you may be motivated after the fourth chapter (Figure to Surround Yourself with Greatness) and then something happens that feels like a big pothole on your path to success. What do you do then? This is what really matters, because you're not going to have an ever-smooth trajectory to your success.

Honestly, when things aren't a bit rough, I'm suspicious. I look at obstacles now as a good challenge, and I thrive on overcoming challenges. Maybe you're this way, as well, but if you are not, if you are the type of person that grows hesitant, clamps up, and becomes afraid, you will have to get over this. When I wrote about fear earlier, I referenced how it can hold you back from everything you wish to accomplish, so remembering this is important.

Look at obstacles as a challenge to prove your worth, and once solved, you'll be more assured you can manage whatever may happen.

Admittedly, the obstacles you may face in a lower price point market are often a bit more challenging than the ones you face with the type of property I mostly work with. More things can go wrong. Sometimes the property may not be in as great of condition or the buyer isn't as secure as thought. I compare this to selling cars, which is obviously an easy reference for me to make. If you are in sales for entry-model cars, you may get thirty people wanting to buy a car a month, and only twelve get financed. Whereas with a luxury vehicle, they mostly all get financed. Homes have these same types of challenges—just in a different market.

By learning the most common obstacles, you can overcome them more easily. This also makes you stand out in your market and people (especially buyers and sellers) are grateful for your knowledge and action. Although they may not admit it, many times an undisciplined realtor is also happy for it, as you're also saving them in a way.

You have to hang in there, and be tough and determined.

THE QUALITY OF RESILIENCE AND CLOSING DEALS

Resilience is built from overcoming obstacles and proving to yourself that they can be conquered.

CHRIS LACHARITY

One of the greatest benefits to obstacles is actually the learning curve and confidence they can bring you. More often than not, when you are meeting with clients face-to-face you have a higher comfort level that is somehow relayed through in your character. The words that reassure a potential client they are talking with a true professional—someone who has their best interests at heart—are present. This matters greatly to clients, because what do they really want: to know their transaction is going to work out and that you have all the details covered. Because they don't care about a realtor's details, they care about the emotions of the transaction. "Don't tell me how it works; make it work."

The best advice I can give anyone who has an obstacle is to avoid talking about having it and start solving it. The rest is just wasted time and psyches you out more than solves anything.

A great way to get a handle on an obstacle is to put it into perspective. Look at it as a personal challenge. Realize that wasting your energy fussing is non-productive and will not do anything to solve what you're facing. Compare what you're up against, let's say, the leader of the country. They are constantly on the go and bombarded with crises to solve and obstacles to conquer. Even though they may have a staff of hundreds helping, the situations are substantially larger in comparison. If that doesn't give you perspective, ask yourself: who am I to complain? The answer—a realtor who wants to get things done! Again, you don't get things done when you are complaining.

Recently, I had a deal worth $4.6 million and the fate of the outcome was in the hands of the lender. The buyer, seller, and the lender kept postponing firming up the deal at various times, which was crazy stressful to everyone else. However, that didn't mean I should clam up and do nothing. I was resilient and kept going with my other tasks and then offered to do what I could to help the lenders, if they needed that assistance.

However, I wasn't about to put all my trust in that lender either. As they figured out things on their end, I began to look at other lenders as a backup plan, if necessary. My ultimate goal is to protect my client and in cases like this, that means making sure I am doing what is best for them. Doing that far outweighed a nice commission. Eventually the deal did close, but it wasn't without hurdle after hurdle, and then the race ended. The checks cleared and it was a done deal. Others involved were exhausted and still talking about the past, but I was thankful to be resilient and focused on the present. In fact, I'd halfway expected it would fall apart despite my efforts and if it did, I would have been okay with that and not felt slighted. It becomes easier to feel that way when you remain on-course by placing someone else's interests before your own.

> **Sticking with clients' best interests will help you in the end and make it so you aren't attached to the commission. You're only dedicated to doing what's right to solve the problems and make sure you are focused on your customer's needs.**

Obstacles come up for every professional because they are not afraid to be on the frontline, taking on the challenges and solving them. My good friend and mentor, Donald Abraham, is a professional like this. He was a commercial realtor, primarily, and he once told me a story of the biggest land deal of his career. It was actually firm when he found something that would hurt his client in the long run. He spoke with colleagues and even his broker, who said: *it's done, don't worry about it.* Being an honest man of high integrity, Donald knew he had to tell his client. That was worth more than the commission. There would always be chances for commissions, but a good client is a gift. He informed his client of his concerns and the deal fell apart. They gave him a "thank you" and he left, glad to have done the right thing but also very aware he'd just lost a six-figure commission. That took great courage.

Donald was the laughing stock of his office for a long time. I cannot fathom how he must have felt, but I do know one thing—he was resilient and better able to handle the ridicule of his peers than he would have been able to handle doing the wrong thing just for a check. One day much later (months, maybe even years), the phone rang and you guessed it, it was the client he protected. "Donald, I have a deal for you," the man said. He shared the details and if it worked out, it would be the largest commission of his career and far more than anyone at his brokerage had ever seen—and definitely earned. Situations like this make me so proud to have Donald as a mentor and a friend. There is no better teacher about the importance of integrity in obstacles, and resilience over easy money.

This story is the way the world works when you want longevity in business. I'm proud to say that I worked the bulk of my career with this man because of his moral compass. Don't be mistaken though; he's an absolute pit bull in business…but, nobody gets hurt in the process.

USE OBSTACLES TO BUILD CHARACTER

Time and dedication to your career will
give you experiences; it's those experiences that give you character.

CHRIS LACHARITY

The single biggest commission of mine to this day is one that came from a series of obstacles with the aforementioned client where I made no commission (but was able to record the two million dollar sale that boosted my sales stats and kickstarted my career in luxury real estate). I had sold their home for over $2M and he said he couldn't afford to pay me if he accepted the deal I'd presented to him. What made this situation trickier was that I represented the buyer, as well, so I had an obligation to them to get them that house, and the offer given truly was all the house was worth. It was in a high sale area, but the owner had overspent when they built it. Many realtors would have walked away, but my obligations to help the owners sell the property and the buyer get the property they wanted didn't allow for that to happen. I did the deal, hoping there might be a few dollars left at the end, but there wasn't—I made zero, but it was still the right thing to do. As fate would have it, there were other complications during that transaction—the seller wasn't happy with what had happened and fired me so the new listing agent also got zero.

Are you wondering why I'd bother? It seems like there was a tremendous amount of anger from the seller toward his situation, and maybe me. Well, it did pay off for me. The seller was able to stay afloat, which was important to him, and then he went on to build an even bigger home. I was involved with that deal and helped extensively, even lending him the deposit. My colleagues thought I'd lost my mind, but all I could remember was my mentor Donald's experience. I had to have faith and keep doing the right thing. It did pay off in the end. This guy built a $3M home, which I double-ended, and I also got to sell the buyer's home for a million bucks too.

This entire transaction worked out because I looked beyond the obstacle in front of me (one that would be easy for some to walk away from) and focused on my obligation as a realtor to help my clients, and that a good deed done is usually rewarded.

The big picture is what you should always keep in mind; commit to staying in a situation for the long haul. For me, this means taking the initiative to learn how to overcome all obstacles to make a name for myself, not just money for my business.

Your reputation is everything when it comes to building up your name and good notoriety in the business. You will always be far better off being a stand-up person who did a deal for free than the one that just walked away from their clients because they were no longer worth their time.

Every experience I have had with a transaction, smooth or otherwise, is also a learning opportunity. Knowing how to relay past experiences to the present day has helped me build my character and has made me prepared for everything that comes my way. I'm not saying I'll never be surprised, but now I have a history of showing I can solve problems when they exist. I'm not saying they never cause a little internal anxiety, but that's for me to deal with, not my clients. To them, I am the one who breaks down obstacles and gets the deal done. I'm there to reassure them things will work out.

THE OBSTACLE OF BALANCE

Creating a balance between your work demands, personal needs, and your social life can be a very complicated situation. I admit, I have myself and Enzo to worry about mostly, which makes my challenges less taxing than they may be for someone with a spouse, a few kids, and other obligations going on outside of work. However, in either case, the focus on trying to find the balance on how to manage all areas of your life is important to your work. I struggle with all of this at different times.

For my personality, these things are my truth:

1. A large part of my work time does cross over into social time, so I rarely feel this pressing desire to just go hang out with my friends socially or go out to eat and forget the "cares of the world."

2. I will take a few hours at least one day a week to just enjoy life and do something I want to do to recharge. That's enough for me, and that is my alone time—this is something that everyone does need, but far too few people take.

3. If I go more than a few days without working out it is not good. My attitude begins to shift and that means my work could suffer, so I am very committed to keeping my workout schedules. In fact, a solid workout can recharge me instantly, and it provides me some great time with my friends who like to work out, as well. This time investment is committed to excellence just as much as any other activity I might do for self-improvement.

For everything that is important to you—and to overcome the obstacles of time and balance—you can solve the problem by creating a schedule where you commit to what you must do for yourself, and then you don't let anything dissuade you from it. You can't do this with everything, of course, but you can do it with things you consider "non-negotiable," such as my workout time.

Along with this topic, it is worth mentioning the obstacles that come from focusing too much on other peoples' successes and what's going on in their careers, therefore distracting you from yours. I am guilty of doing this sometimes. When I hear about another realtor who makes more money than I do, I begin to compare myself to them. Once in a while, I'll slip up and it will deflate me. That's when those overly tough, critical voices come out and try to doubt me.

When you are too critical of yourself, you become your own worst enemy.

If you are susceptible to being influenced by other peoples' successes, be mindful you do not want it to become a deterrent to your own plans for success. If you follow these guidelines, it will help:

1. See if there is something you can learn or extract from their successes.
2. Realize that everyone has a different path to success and you don't know their full story (struggles, lessons, etc.) so it is a waste of time to compare. Just be the best you!

Ultimately, you don't want to be envious of anyone and you should be happy for everyone who does well. If anything, they are evidence there is room for success. Pursue your dreams, and that is the healthiest thing you can do for your mind and career.

One of my favorite things to do is ask people how they do certain things, and try to learn from them. There are many people willing to share their experiences with you—if you just ask. Recently, I asked a friend if I could do a podcast with him. He has a successful podcast and I'd never done one. I wanted to see what it was like. It proved to be a fantastic experience that sparked a new idea in me that resonated with me strongly. It would be a dream opportunity for me to interview successful people for podcasts. I could see myself doing it, and if I had not understood how a podcast worked, that could have been an obstacle. But I took the uncertainty away, learned a bit, and now I have a new dream to add to my thoughts. Just because I love real estate doesn't mean I will ever stop growing into other areas of interest.

Being singular in your focus for too long will turn into an obstacle. You have to look around you, not just at the one thing in front of you at that moment.

MANAGING TIME WASTERS

There's no good way to waste your time.
Wasting time is just wasting time.

HELEN MIRREN

The topic of dealing with those individuals who want a lot of your time, but are not really going anywhere has come up a few times in this book. But what about the obstacle of someone dominating your time and attention when a parade of other potential clients is going past you? This can happen frequently during open houses for realtors (mostly new realtors).

When you first begin in real estate, you are going to be eager to build up your networking list and hopefully get the chance to prove yourself to new clients. A great way to grow this list is by hosting an open house. Some realtors host open houses for their entire career, but most, once their success begins to rise, will hand off those opportunities to new realtors. People may come in and you greet them, give them information, sign the book (if you have one), ask if they have any questions, and also see if they are under contract with any other realtor. Then, one of these scenarios may play out:

1. They look around the house and sneak out without making so much as eye contact with you;
2. They take a look around and come back to ask you questions;
3. Or, they begin a conversation with you (before or after looking) that keeps on going and going.

The last reference is the one you need to worry about. That obstacle could lead to you not getting the touches with potential other clients you are seeking. You have to let people understand your time is valuable and while you want to be helpful to them, unless they are the only people in the house, you should make sure you don't skip a beat with the other guests.

There is nothing wrong with excusing yourself so you can introduce yourself to someone else. It's not rude and if by chance someone doesn't understand that, it's better to know that right away, because they may not be the client you want. Just because you're learning how to handle obstacles doesn't mean you want to willingly take them on, after all! A difficult client can be an expensive client.

If someone feels they are the only Coca-Cola in the desert, they may be hard to deal with.

If you are genuinely polite, you can dismiss yourself without any concerns, but when you are overly polite and allow people to dictate your time, you'll run into some problems.

Here are a few additional options you can do to maintain control of your time in all situations:

1. **Let the person(s) you are talking with know you have to go and you would like to schedule a time to talk further with them.**
   What's great about this strategy is: 1) you stay on schedule; and 2) you can tell if they are really a serious potential client. If they aren't, they won't want that appointment to talk further.

2. **Don't overbook yourself.**

   Too many appointments scheduled too tightly together create challenges for you that can lead to: 1) you running late for your next appointment, which is likely to throw you off your best game; and 2) you may sound rushed and uncaring when you talk with the client who is right in front of you. Neither of these scenarios are good.

3. **Don't just drive people around looking at homes without a commitment.**

   Not all agents are great at getting a Buyer's Representation Agreement, which is the document that shows a buyer is committed to working with you to purchase a property. With this document, if they end up going rogue and using another agent to purchase a home, you'll still get paid. Thankfully, this doesn't happen too often, but I recommend you get one before you invest a day or multiple days running clients around to look at a bunch of properties. Not everyone will be honest about working with another realtor, but if you bring in a document like the BRA, they are likely to be truthful.

   Another option when using a BRA is that if I do get a call that someone wants to look at a property right away, and I may have the time to accommodate their needs, I'll ask them the standard question: are you working with another agent? If they say "no," I'll reply, "Great. I am going to generate a BRA just for this property in case you decide you'd like to purchase it." At that point, they either are glad to agree or forced to come clean and admit they are working with another agent. And if they are serious, they'll call their agent. Either way, I cleared up the value of my time in a matter of minutes. Some people find this to be bold, but I find it to be smart. You have to value your time or no one else will.

   Your time is one of your greatest assets and you should never feel bad or awkward about using it to your best professional advantage. In the end, you'll save yourself many headaches and stresses, plus experience many more victories on your journey to success, if you are aware of how you manage your time.

FIGURE TO DO THESE 3 THINGS

When it comes to overcoming obstacles, my best teachers have been some of my greatest mentors—like Donald Abraham. He is always cool under pressure and his underlying reasoning isn't based on emotions, but solutions. The three suggestions I have for you are based on what I've seen in him throughout the years and have worked to implement into my own life.

1. **Don't be thrown off your game when an obstacle comes your way.**
    It's not that you want to expect obstacles and troubles to come your way, but if you are building a career in real estate it is almost inevitable. Transactions involve a lot of people and details, some of which you can control and some of which you cannot. By being a thorough and diligent agent, you'll be able to handle and predict a lot of things you have control over (inspections, appraised values, etc.). However, for those other things not within your "realtor scope," you should still be the positive voice of reason that works to find understanding, answers, and a solution.

2. **Avoid the panic button.**
    Calm yourself down and find resolution. If I'm doing something for myself, I find I don't handle it as well as if I'm doing it for someone else. So, if I am in this situation, I'll actually visualize I am solving someone else's problem and by doing that I tend to give calmer, better advice to overcome the obstacle and move on.

3. **Stick to the "is that all you've got" line of thinking.**
    When you stay in this frame of mind, it's empowering to you and how you process everything that happens to you. It is a reminder that you

are not dealing with the worst thing ever, but an obstacle that you can overcome by using your skills and talents as a deal maker.

I hope you took a lot of great insight away to help you stay on track, even when obstacles are on your course. Don't let anything or anyone get in your way. Life has a way of constantly trying to distract you, and it's persistent. No matter what your goals are, commit to them and don't let friends, colleagues, family, or anyone dissuade you.

> The harder the conflict, the more glorious the triumph. What we obtain too cheap, we esteem too lightly; it is dearness only that gives everything its value. I love the man that can smile in trouble, that can gather strength from distress and grow.

> ———————————

> **THOMAS PAIN**

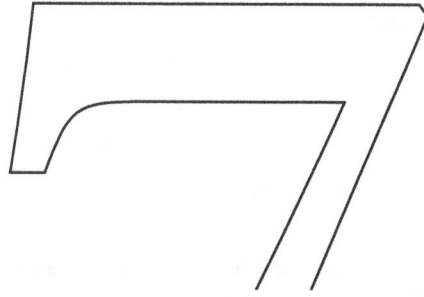

FIGURE TO SEND THE ELEVATOR BACK DOWN

Life is no brief candle to me. It is a sort of splendid torch which I have got a hold of for the moment, and I want to make it burn as brightly as possible before handing it on to future generations.

GEORGE BERNARD SHAW

T his is simple: when you find success, you should help others. It's satisfying to achieve something significant in your life and then help others do the same in theirs. Although I am not where I want to be with my goals—yet—I still realize the power of this, and find some of my greatest inspiration takes place when I reach out to help someone else who wants help.

There is plenty of business to go around and people won't forget you took the time to help them out and to show you believed in them.

It's my greatest hope that my adventure whilst writing this book to achieve a massive goal will inspire you, and also open up more opportunities for me to begin coaching people who want to escalate their career in some capacity. It may not be fully in place right now, but it is in the process of happening, and I cannot wait! Why? Because "I'm hungry," as my mentor Les Brown says.

When someone else is looking up to you, you cannot let that person down. You also open up a personal opportunity for you to learn something. It's a great cycle, which helps everyone out. For me, listening to Les Brown is a constant source of inspiration. I never get sick of it and if you're a passenger in my car, you have a good chance of hearing him speak.

Always remember… Success breeds success.

THE GIFTS OF OFFERING YOUR WISDOM

What I have always responded to most
about sending the elevator back down is that
helping others feels good, and it is a way to
feel grateful for what I've gained expertise in.

CHRIS LACHARITY

You cannot be an effective mentor, teacher, coach, inspiration, or whatever you'd like to term it, to someone else if your heart and a genuine interest in helping isn't a part of the equation. I find this to be refreshing and it feels good. This type of emotion creates the type of energy that makes me work through challenging days—compared to the "will this day ever end" thoughts. You can't be into helping others with the expectation of something in return, because that wouldn't be a great intention. However, you can give of your time and talents to people who show they are hungry for more, and believe you can teach them. What greater compliment could there be?

Even when I was younger and not readily willing to accept advice, I always felt that when a professional or someone I admired gave me their opinion and perspective on something, it was like a breath of fresh air. Why wouldn't I give credit to it? After all, they had already done, experienced, and lived things I was still striving to achieve (or avoid).

Imagine the potential stemming from that...

If you invest your time in someone just starting out in real estate that you recognize potential in, or see your younger self in, you could very well be training someone that becomes a star performer for your team someday. Or they hit it big in other ways. The point is, they don't forget you and what you do for them, any more than you forget them and what they've done for you. Everyone wins, and you cannot be successful in your own life if you are fearful of others becoming more successful than you. You don't determine winners and losers; people who want to grow their careers and achieve goals determine if they are going to be the winner or loser.

You can work hard at your career and succeed on your own, but you can make the experience more rewarding by finding someone you can rely on to help you figure out how to define your best course for that moment. A great coach and mentor will help you understand challenges, make better decisions, and also get you to understand who you are—and what you're made of.

As busy as I am, I find great joy in being able to answer a person's questions or give them an encouraging nudge whenever I can. It is always worth the time and if someone is sincere, taking the time to ask me a question about their career, or something that I do for success, I will give them a sincere and forthright answer—nothing less than this is deserved.

How about you? Do you have people you can rely on that have proven experience and exude the qualities that have been laid out in this book? If you don't, make sure you start seeking those who show greatness in their craft—even if it isn't real estate. Any person in any field can provide something of value to you if you open up your mind to it. Just recently, I went to give a sales seminar at a fitness club chain, sharing with their staff how they could ask for referrals and make sales comfortably. That was a rewarding experience for me, as well as another opportunity to share why I am so passionate about the "people helping people" connection that's so important to this world.

5 POWERFUL MENTORING TIPS

One of the greatest values of mentors
is the ability to see ahead what others
cannot see and to help them navigate
a course to their destination.

JOHN C. MAXWELL

When it comes to strategic mentoring, you cannot help everyone who may ask you for help. There is a certain bit of discernment you can take advantage of on your end to ensure you are actually working with someone who wants to benefit from your attention. Not that you want them to blindly agree with your every word and action, but you do want someone that shows they are engaged in the entire process. This is important, because if you spread yourself too thinly to too many people who are not prepared for what you have to offer, no one will be ahead and your satisfaction with the experience will be lessened.

If you're wondering why you should worry about you mentoring at this point, I want you to realize that even at this stage of your career, and with aspirations of your own in progress, you are fully capable of helping someone else. You have strengths that others do not, just as those mentors you seek out have strengths that you do not. That is part of what makes it a valuable win-win proposition. You can't get much better deal than that.

1. **Realize it is okay to be wrong.**
    I have come to realize that you have to be humble to be coached. If you are not, you are going to struggle with someone showing you different ways to do things. I had someone work for me who claimed they wanted

to soak in everything I had to offer, but every time I'd suggest something or try to explain why they may consider an alternative approach, they refused to take the information. What did that tell me? They said that they wanted mentorship and to learn, but they were more attached to their own thoughts and beliefs of how certain things should work. This person didn't stick around long in the end, and I do hope that someday they'll find the humility they need in order to truly benefit from a mentor.

2. **Don't go into a mentoring relationship with the mindset that you are going to "change" someone.**

    A mentor is like a trusted advisor, someone who provides guidance, motivation and moral support, a role model. Someone you will occasionally go to for advice on how to progress and be more successful in the same area as the mentor. The goal of the mentor is to bring the mentee up to where the mentor is at the time, either following a similar path or advising them on doing certain things differently, based on their learning experience. In other words a mentors' job is to change the mentees' mindset.

3. **Asking versus offering is important to consider.**

    A good mentoring relationship comes from the one you are mentoring choosing to ask questions that will help them learn and grow and form their own educated opinions. You can just offer wisdom and tell people what to do, of course, but many people are resistant to advice they didn't solicit. Another consideration is if someone continues to ask you what they should do, but they never do it, don't continue to feed them extensive time, energy, and ideas. It's like shouting into a canyon—all you're going to get in response is your own echo.

4. **Create conversations and opportunities to get feedback from whomever you mentor.**

    It's exciting and educational for a mentor to get feedback on how something they suggested turned out when tried. This should be very important to you, and if you engage in a sincere conversation about what's been learned through the advice you offered, you will likely learn something too. For example, if what you suggested didn't quite work out the way you thought it would and the one you're mentoring adapted something to make it work, you should be as proud as a parent on graduation day. Plus, that information exchange has also given you something new to consider. It's a great reminder of why both parties involved in mentorship thrive.

5. **As a mentor, you can assist in creating meaningful goals and strategies.**
   Different people set goals in different ways. Some go so big they toss themselves out of contention because they don't have a big plan to match it. Other people go so small they are achieving one goal every month, easily. Don't kid yourself—that is no goal, which is why a mentor can help you to see greater potential in yourself.

All of these reasons to mentor and what to expect from that type of relationship should resonate with you in two ways:

1. what may be expected of you if someone gives you the gift of mentorship;
2. in what ways can you expect to build up someone else's life through your gift of mentorship.

Through mentorship:

1. Loyalties are built;
2. Character is defined;
3. Fulfillment is recognized;
4. Selflessness is expressed;
5. Lives are improved;
6. And, success is cultivated.

How can you not love all that? Send the elevator down, please!

LEARNING THROUGH PARTICIPATION

One of the most effective ways
to learn is to shadow your mentor
and watch them 'in action'.

CHRIS LACHARITY

Don't assume you have to block out time for mentoring, because there are other options you can do. You can either answer a quick question or call, and then get back to your tasks and be highly effective. Unless coaching or mentoring is going to be your career, blocking out hours of your income-earning time is not typically wise. However, having someone that wants to watch you in action can be a very effective way for someone to learn—as long as they don't delay going off and trying these things on their own stream of business.

Many people have shadowed me when I'm at work with clients. Some of them have had a few years' experience and were looking to improve their skills. Others were just starting out. I appreciate the opportunity to help all these people, and my clients never mind their presence, either. I think it shows (without having to express it) my expertise—and that is valuable to express in as many ways as possible.

However, I have had the occasional person who never stopped shadowing me. They were resistant to launch out on their own, and that is not a sign of effective mentorship—that is a sign they are really just using up time, not improving themselves through time well spent. When this happens, I seldom have to say anything to that type of individual, because eventually they will grow bored or realize they have to start finding a way to make money. For those who stick it out, though, and begin to take initiatives on their own, I find great value in them for helping me with my business. Everyone wins.

One of my favorite stories is when I tried to mentor someone and it went in a surprising and unexpected direction. I had a young guy who worked for me—let's call him Steve.

When I held boardroom meetings to motivate my team, we'd all gather around and try to generate excitement. It usually focused on trying to create a big push for the end of the month and get a few more deals closed in the books. Everyone would throw out their numbers for what they could potentially close for the month. Maybe six, five, four...something like that. But not Steve. His answer was always "one."

I was always frustrated his goals were so low, but I couldn't get through to him to think bigger. Yet, since he was a family connection, I never wanted to give up. In my office, I had a Galileo thermometer that was kind of a traveling trophy that went to the realtor who reached their goals every month. Of course, Steve got it every month because he set low goals. But was that impressive? No, of course not.

In an effort to motivate Steve to "think bigger," I incorporated his help one month with a client, because I had to head to Toronto. I told him if he let some clients into a house they wanted to look at and they bought it, I'd pay him $10K. Well, sure enough they purchased it. Steve was so excited and I was so hopeful.

Then, Steve had a total shift and everyone said he turned into a mini-me. He was super excited, pumped, and positive about real estate. Then shortly after, Steve went to Thailand to find himself. He was a star for about a month, and then that was the end of his career with us. Today, he works for a discount broker giving his services away for practically nothing.

What an experience that was. I chuckle about it today, but there are some key lessons in there that really apply to the desire to mentor compared to the desire to use mentorship to excel in life. You can see someone that you think has potential and reach out, but if they don't have a pure heart for what they're doing and motivation, you can't make it happen for them. I still think Steve has potential, but he has now surrounded himself with like-minded people who feel their services aren't worth much.

You can only take a person as far as they're willing to go.

Live and learn…just don't stop.

OTHER WAYS TO GIVE BACK

There are numerous ways to give back to your community. This is a worthwhile investment both emotionally and in the physical community itself, a stronger community is a better community for everyone to work and live in. So, in this regard, sending the elevator back down also has to do with your spirit of giving.

Our world has different types of givers. There are those that let everyone know they gave this amount of money to some organization or event; and then there are those that are "silent givers." I personally prefer to be a silent giver, knowing that karma and good energy will reward me for those efforts in due time. And even if they didn't, it wouldn't matter, because I have the means to offer something to make someone else's life better. That feels pretty spectacular.

We make a living by what we get.
We make a life by what we give.

WINSTON CHURCHILL

One time when I was out with my uncle, I saw the practice of silent charity in action, and it really inspired me on many levels. He had slipped a hundred dollars on the sly to someone who needed money. He saw no one was looking and when he returned to the table, he didn't say a word about it. That I admire. I don't admire the person who would have done that and come back to the table and bragged about it. Doing that just takes away from the good intention of the gesture, in my opinion.

I don't send the elevator back down to get something from it, other than that feeling that I get inside. If the word of what you did is going to get out, don't let it be from you—allow others to sincerely spread that word because they choose to.

FIGURE TO DO THESE 3 THINGS

In the world of real estate, helping each other is what makes a difference. Those who are willing to help each other out, through mentoring and being mentored, will create a stronger core group of professionals that can be real difference makers—not only in their clients' lives, but in the lives of people, in general. Always strive to be that type of individual.

1. **Remember where you came from.**
    Instead of being an egotistical jerk, remember you were just starting out at one time too. Give others the benefit of the doubt and be excited for them that they are starting a new journey and you can participate in it.

2. **Don't assume the role of the "all-knowing."**
    Instead of saying, "I've been doing this work a long time, listen to me," open up your mind when mentoring because if done properly, it'll be a two-way street.

3. **Recognize ways you can mentor without overspending your valuable time.**
    There is a good balance to achieve between helping others and continuing with your goals. Ideally, the two will always complement each other and work for both parties. It's worth the time to figure out the equation that makes this work in your life, as it's a place where great personal rewards exist.

True fulfillment is in acceptance and appreciation. True fulfillment lies in the journey, not just the endpoint. True fulfillment is life itself.

CANDACE THOTH

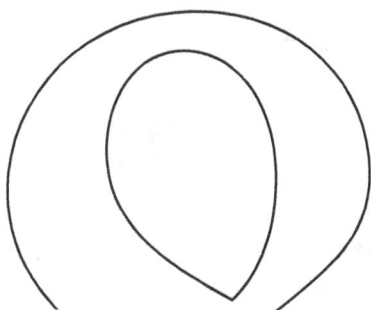

INVESTING IN YOU

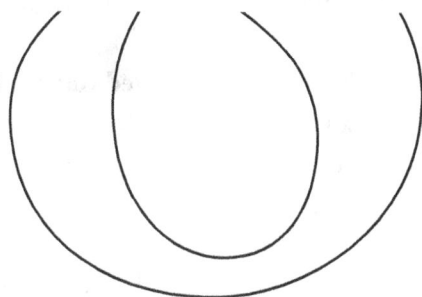

The best investment in your growth will not be disguised in sugar-coated, 'feel-good' words. It will be revealed through bold statements that show tangible actions you can take to succeed.

CHRIS LACHARITY

You've learned a lot of things from me—a guy who knows a lot and continues to learn a lot—but equally importantly, a guy who is still taking the journey. I'm not reflecting on "days long past" and offering you advice I am not forced to take myself each and every day to make my goal. We're in this together, which feels kind of good to me, and I hope it does to you too!

If you want to make your real estate career work for you, it's important to educate yourself and then take some massive, bold action to see if what you've learned actually works. Consider it the "street smarts" of real estate, compared to just being "book smart" about the concepts that exist. The combination of both is the sweet spot where you'll find your success. Pretty awesome.

You need to strive to be the most prepared you can be. The time will come when you can wing it if needed, but by that time, you'll have stats and success to back you up. Then it becomes an entirely different game.

The key to it all is to do what you need to do to be a professional. A professional is spotted by:

1. Sharing what they know confidently;
2. Knowing where to seek out what they don't know quickly and efficiently;
3. And, knowing that continuous learning is the only way to create continuous success.

If you commit to becoming this person, you can succeed in everything you set your mind to, whether it's real estate or another aspiration you have. This sounds simple, and it is simple—even when life gets complicated.

There are a few ways to create this mastery in your own life, and it's a combination of your actions in your target market, and reaching out for more information and education when you find it to be necessary. This means you:

1. **Learn how to get the proper benefits from seminars you attend**
    Being a professional seminar-goer will give you lots of information to store in your brain, but it does little to work for you if you don't go out and take action to achieve your goals.

2. **Find the best sources of motivation and inspiration for your life**
    Motivation can last a little amount of time or a long time. You could attend an event and leave so motivated to conquer the world, just to lose that motivation with the first distraction that meets you along the way. Inspiration, however, comes from the heart and it is a commitment you make through your mind and actions that reminds you exactly why you are doing what you've set out to do.

3. **Commit to 7 Figures to Success…do not accept any other number**
    Each of the 7 Figures to Success is one that is applicable to some aspect of your personal growth or career development. They work best when they are all working together and are the guide to get you to your goals—even goals that are 7 figures!

> Desire is the key to motivation, but it's determination and commitment to an unrelenting pursuit of your goal—a commitment to excellence—that will enable you to attain the success you seek.
>
> MARIO ANDRETTI

7 FIGURES TO FILL YOUR CUP

For many days and years before writing this book, I've worked to improve myself with these 7 figures, just as every day since writing this book, I have still been diligent in committing to them.

It has not taken extra time.

It has produced results.

It has kept me in the frame of mind I need to be in for success.

It has been one day at a time. Now, it's your turn!

#1: Figure to Be Kind

I cannot think of a situation that can help you grow professionally or experience true fulfillment personally where you toss aside kindness for any other thought or action. You can avoid being taken advantage of and not lose your kindness. You can show kindness in times when other people do not. It doesn't have to be optional or "one or the other."

#2: Figure to Ride the Wave

Since the real estate industry is considered cyclical, you need to be smart about how you approach your day-to-day endeavors. Follow a system, don't celebrate a big success by stopping what you did to earn it, and be grateful for business that comes your way when you least expect it.

#3: Figure to be in it for the Long Haul

Success and mastery do not come from a lack of dedication, and when you are truly interested in growing a career in real estate, you don't want to be put in the group that are known as the "dabblers." You want to show you are committed to what you are doing, and it is your career priority. Night and weekend hours alone do not cut it. Have faith in yourself, and don't be hesitant to throw yourself into the fray and do what it takes to come out winning!

#4: Figure to Surround Yourself with Greatness

What you do, combined with whom you associate with, is who you truly are. This means there cannot really be separation of your private life from your professional life when it comes to your values, ethics, and associations when you are living in a success mindset and figuring on great things for your life. Be mindful of this, and you'll find incredible opportunities with difference makers and deal creators coming your way—and you'll truly enjoy the company of these types of people, as well.

#5: Figure to Cut the BS

As Steve Maraboli said: "At the end of the day, let there be no excuses, no explanations, no regrets." You have to be honest with yourself about what you are doing, and if what you are doing doesn't match with what you are saying, cut the BS and be authentic.

#6: Figure to Overcome Obstacles

If you think you can go through life without obstacles or challenges, either you are doing yourself a big injustice by kidding yourself, or you are not striving for anything great in your life. Everyone has obstacles on the road to success, and all of them should become lessons that pave your path to greatness.

#7: Figure to Send the Elevator Back Down

The ultimate reward of your success is more than just achievement and perhaps a financial gain; it is the ability to use what you've learned to help someone else who is beginning their journey, or just needs assistance. When you send the elevator back down you are giving another person a wonderful opportunity if that person is willing to get into that elevator. Be wise and smart about whom you offer this service to professionally, and when you have an opportunity to give to someone in need, do so humbly and quietly. You don't need to say a word, because a good action of that magnitude does not go unnoticed.

If you've ever wanted to figure on anything in your life, why not figure on you being able to make the biggest difference? No, it isn't just you alone. It's a combination of clients, mentors, associates, and life experiences that define your life, but no one can make the most of your experience for you!

The celebration...you cannot practice it or anything. It's a moment when the excitement of your goal makes you react to the moment.

PETER BONDRA

I have to admit I never factored emotional stress into my goals this year. I had the hardest time dealing with certain decisions I made going into the year that deeply affected my thoughts and performance. There were times I didn't even care about my goal. Maybe those words resonate with you because at some time your own plans were in danger of being derailed. Maybe you're going through something now that is holding you back.

I had many days where I was extremely saddened by my regret of hurting someone very close to me. I couldn't reverse the damage I caused no matter how hard I tried. It lived with me every day throughout this year and changed me as a person. I know in the end it was a hard lesson for me to learn but necessary to make sure I never lost my awareness of someone else's feelings and to be in touch with my own. I didn't see what was most important standing right in front of me.

I felt a need to share a vulnerable side of me so that I could be more relatable to you whilst reading this. We all have our own stuff to deal with and it can be overwhelming. I noticed as I read some great books and listened to podcast interviews with successful people who shared their struggles and showed vulnerability instead of only their wins that I wasn't alone. This gave me hope that all would work out if I could just hold it together and keep moving toward my goal. It became less and less about financial gain and more about achieving something I could be proud of and build upon. Working on myself and becoming a better person along the way has helped me further appreciate life, which in turn has helped me appreciate those close to me even more.

Don't beat yourself up for not learning something sooner that you didn't know existed.

> Don't let anything stand in the way
> of you claiming and manifesting the
> life that you choose rather than
> the life you have by default.

JOY PAGE

My goal whilst writing this book has been to have a million-dollar-commission year; a big hearty goal that would take all my energy and drive to even attempt to bring to fruition. For me, this is a worthy goal to cement everything I've practiced and written here, into existence. Writing this book held me accountable to my goal once I committed to it, so thank you. By reading this book, you have helped give me the energy to keep going for this. Let's face it; I've cast it out there and now my feet are to the fire. I've carried this with me every month and some stress and self-induced anxiety have come my way because of it. But I've managed to deal with that and grow stronger because of it. I was interested in telling this story in hopes it might inspire someone else to incorporate some of my beliefs and theories in order to achieve their goals. I welcome you to contact me if I can offer any guidance along your journey.

I'm pursuing a goal that only about 10 realtors out of 3,000 have achieved. So, no matter how great your game is, it isn't easy. It takes discipline and belief.

Out of that elite group of successful people, I know most of them and how hard they've worked to achieve what they have. They've inspired me in many ways—sometimes showing me what to avoid and other times giving me some insight into what to do. You can't sacrifice your life and wellbeing to achieve goals, which is important for me to remember. I didn't want to recognize this big goal in my early forties just to be exhausted, worn, and haggard. This is why I stress the importance in appreciating what you have while remaining driven and take care of your health since without it you have nothing. I wouldn't have the energy to do what I do if I didn't hit the gym consistently. Enjoy your body, enjoy your surroundings and enjoy your journey.

One day in retrospect, the years of struggle will strike you as the most beautiful

---

SIGMUND FREUD

It's November and I'm pressing 'send' to my publisher, on track for my goal. I have a good 6 weeks to make some serious money but I have no doubt I'll make it. Even if I come close, all the rules still apply however I'm hitting it! If you see me or contact me, feel free to ask if I hit the one million…I will gladly respond with a resounding yes!

I speak this way because although I doubted myself at times, I've remained confident this is possible. Like Brian Buffini says, "Most people aim at nothing and hit it with tremendous accuracy."

If you adopted my philosophy and aimed for a million dollars next year and that mindset brought you to $750,000, would that not be a tremendous success? What do you have to lose?

I always found it fascinating that people in real estate hit a figure like $250,000 per year and stay there. They even say I make $250k a year and seem to always make, give or take very close to that amount. That's because that's the value they have placed on themselves. My new value is one million so that's what I make per year. I might try and double it again to $2 million, but I know I won't go below that from now on because that's my new number. This is just as possible for you as it is for me. Just reprogram your mind with your new number and get to work.

That's the best advice I could finish off with. I really think it's as simple as that. The only thing that could possibly stand in your way is you.

And now a new chapter begins…

ABOUT CHRIS LACHARITY

C hris has enjoyed a prosperous career in real estate coming from a successful background of high end car sales with Mercedes Benz. Dealing with Ottawa's elite naturally brought him into luxury real estate. He formed his own sales team and has consistently enjoyed much success and ranked at the top of his profession year after year.

As a representative of Engel & Völkers, Chris Lacharity merges his passions for architecture and design with a love of making a positive impact on people's lives. With 20 years experience of high-end sales comes a large network of clientele. Combining this vast network of high-end clients matching Ottawa's most elite with the finest homes the Capital has to offer, and his association with Engel & Völkers, the connections, reach and drive is unbeatable.

Chris has helped hundreds of happy clients buy, sell and invest. He believes in being relational not transactional, looking at the big picture forming long lasting and loyal relationships with his clients.

His positive, invigorated approach appeals to new and experienced homebuyers wishing to navigate complex real estate processes in an easily understandable fashion. He is definitely no stranger to multi-million dollar deals and recognizes one must do whatever it takes to close a deal successfully. Chris strongly believes "you are only as good as you are today" and strives for constant improvement. If you were to meet him, you would surely hear him say "it's never about the agent, it's always about the best interests of the client."

Originally from Ottawa, Chris has a vast knowledge of the area and is well versed in all areas of the market.

Together with his reputation and the marketing of Engel & Völkers, buyers and sellers of Ottawa luxury real estate can be assured Chris provides the best possible results for new and experienced homebuyers and sellers alike.

"Every property is somebody's dream!"

CONTACT CHRIS LACHARITY

ChrisLacharity.com
Chris@chrislacharity.com
613 240 8609
@chrislacharity

FIGURES TO
SUCCESS

JOURNAL

If found please contact:

_____

_____

_____

7 FIGURES TO SUCCESS JOURNAL

Date_____/_____/_____

My top three goals for today are:

1. _____

2. _____

3. _____

My top three massive action steps to achieve my daily goals are:

1. _____

2. _____

3. _____

My daily affirmation for today:

I am super grateful and happy not that I ... _____

_____

_____

_____

_____

My daily revenue goal in order to achieve my annual revenue goal is:

$. _____

7 FIGURES TO SUCCESS JOURNAL

Date_____/_____/_____

My top three goals for today are:

1. _____
2. _____
3. _____

My top three massive action steps to achieve my daily goals are:

1. _____
2. _____
3. _____

My daily affirmation for today:

I am super grateful and happy not that I ... _____

_____

_____

_____

_____

My daily revenue goal in order to achieve my annual revenue goal is:

$. _____

7 FIGURES TO SUCCESS JOURNAL

Date _____/_____/_____

My top three goals for today are:

1. _____
2. _____
3. _____

My top three massive action steps to achieve my daily goals are:

1. _____
2. _____
3. _____

My daily affirmation for today:

I am super grateful and happy not that I ... _____

_____

_____

_____

_____

My daily revenue goal in order to achieve my annual revenue goal is:

$. _____

7 FIGURES TO SUCCESS JOURNAL

Date _____/_____/_____

My top three goals for today are:

1. _____

2. _____

3. _____

My top three massive action steps to achieve my daily goals are:

1. _____

2. _____

3. _____

My daily affirmation for today:

I am super grateful and happy not that I ... _____

_____

_____

_____

_____

My daily revenue goal in order to achieve my annual revenue goal is:

$. _____

7 FIGURES TO SUCCESS JOURNAL

Date _____/_____/_____

My top three goals for today are:

1. _____
2. _____
3. _____

My top three massive action steps to achieve my daily goals are:

1. _____
2. _____
3. _____

My daily affirmation for today:

I am super grateful and happy not that I ... _____

_____

_____

_____

_____

My daily revenue goal in order to achieve my annual revenue goal is:

$. _____

7 FIGURES TO SUCCESS JOURNAL

Date _____/_____/_____

My top three goals for today are:

1. _____
2. _____
3. _____

My top three massive action steps to achieve my daily goals are:

1. _____
2. _____
3. _____

My daily affirmation for today:

I am super grateful and happy not that I ... _____

_____

_____

_____

_____

My daily revenue goal in order to achieve my annual revenue goal is:

$. _____

7 FIGURES TO SUCCESS JOURNAL

Date_____/_____/_____

My top three goals for today are:

1. _____

2. _____

3. _____

My top three massive action steps to achieve my daily goals are:

1. _____

2. _____

3. _____

My daily affirmation for today:

I am super grateful and happy not that I ... _____

_____

_____

_____

_____

My daily revenue goal in order to achieve my annual revenue goal is:

$. _____

7 FIGURES TO SUCCESS JOURNAL

Date_____/_____/_____

My top three goals for today are:

1. _____
2. _____
3. _____

My top three massive action steps to achieve my daily goals are:

1. _____
2. _____
3. _____

My daily affirmation for today:

I am super grateful and happy not that I ... _____

_____

_____

_____

_____

My daily revenue goal in order to achieve my annual revenue goal is:

$. _____

Trust is such an important factor in choosing a realtor because, if they don't have your best interests at heart throughout the entire selling process, the biggest asset you likely have will be at serious risk. Chris and his team made us feel that selling our home was their top priority. They were accessible at any time of the day or night and, with their combined wisdom and expertise in the high-end market, were wizards at achieving the best sales outcome on our behalves. These folks are the real deal in real estate and we highly recommend them to anyone who wants to be on the winning end of selling their home!

Drs Kevin and Susan Goheen

CHRIS LACHARITY

Selling Lifestyle in Ottawa for Record Value
Year After Year

ENGEL&VÖLKERS®

CHRIS LACHARITY

Sales Representative

Direct: 613-240-8609
Chris@ChrisLacharity.com

ENGEL&VÖLKERS®
CHRIS LACHARITY TEAM

Engel & Völkers Ottawa Central, Brokerage. Independently owned & operated.

www.ingramcontent.com/pod-product-compliance
Lightning Source LLC
Chambersburg PA
CBHW070656190326
41458CB00052B/6908/J